Preface

Administering Microsoft Azure SQL Solutions DP 300: 250+ Practice Questions is a meticulously curated resource designed to support candidates preparing for the DP-300 certification exam. This book serves as a comprehensive guide for database administrators and IT professionals, providing an extensive collection of practice questions, multiple-choice questions (MCQs) from previous years, and real-world scenarios that align with the essential competencies required for Microsoft Azure SQL solutions. Covering a broad spectrum of topics, including Azure SQL Database, Azure SQL Managed Instance, and SQL Server on Azure Virtual Machines (both Windows and Linux), this book offers a structured approach to mastering the operational aspects of cloud-native and hybrid data platform solutions built on SQL Server and Azure SQL services. Through its well-structured content, candidates will gain a deep understanding of critical areas such as database management, availability, security, performance optimization, and automation using Transact-SQL (T-SQL) and administrative tools.

This book is more than just a compilation of practice questions—it is a strategic learning tool designed to reinforce knowledge, identify areas requiring further study, and simulate real exam conditions. The detailed explanations accompanying each question provide valuable insights, helping candidates develop a clear and practical understanding of key concepts. Whether you are an experienced database professional seeking certification validation or a newcomer aspiring to establish expertise in Azure database administration, DP-300 Administering Microsoft Azure SQL Solutions: 250+ Practice Questions serves as a definitive guide to enhance your readiness and confidence for the DP-300 examination. Engage with the content, challenge yourself with the questions, and let this book be your trusted companion in achieving success in Microsoft Azure SQL administration.

Table of Contents

Chapter 1: Part 1

1. You have a Microsoft Azure SQL server virtual machine. You wish to install log shipping such that you could store backups on a dedicated SMTP file share. You need to configure servers to perform the Log Shipping step. Which server instance would you choose to configure and perform actions such as complete backup job & copy backup Job You can choose the same server instance for different actions performed?
A. Monitor Server Instance
B. Primary Server Instance
C. Secondary Server Instance
D. Backup Share file Server

Correct Answers: B, C

2. I want to compress my table dbo.myTable. I start with the following code:
• ALTER TABLE dbo.myTable
• REBUILD PARTITION = ALL
• WITH (DATA_COMPRESSION =
Which of the options is NOT a valid ending to this code?
A. PAGE)
B. ROW)
C. NONE)
D. PREFIX)

Correct Answer: D

3. You plan to create a table in an Azure Synapse Analytics dedicated SQL pool. The data in the table is invoice data under the sales schema for the past 3 years. SQL Monitor has raised a "Long running query" which when executed showed details about all invoices generated over years to gather month-wise sales for individual items. Due to this management decided to purge data, once a year for data that is older than three years.
Using which of the options below can you ensure that data can be distributed evenly across partitions such that the operation of purging data is accelerated?
A. Filegroup
B. Partition scheme
C. Partition Function
D. Partition Column

Correct Answer: C

4. You have an Azure SQL server virtual machine.
You need to back up the transaction log from the Primary server instance to the secondary server instance. Which option should you choose?
A. Implement 'Always On' availability groups
B. Configure transactional replication

C. Configure Transaction Log Shipping
D. Import a DACPAC

Correct Answer: C

5. You have a large production Azure SQL database named 'bankdb'. You are running a reporting or analytics workload on this data that is causing performance issues.
To overcome this issue you decide to have a second database such that additional workload can be handled thereby minimizing the performance impact on your production workload. Data Sync helps you to keep the two databases synchronized. Below are the steps required to set up SQL Data Sync between databases. Identify the correct sequence from the options below.
A. Add a Database in Azure SQL Database
B. Add a SQL Server Database
C. Create a Sync group
D. Configure Sync Group
E. Add Sync Member

Correct Answer: C, E, A, B and D

6. You have an Azure subscription.
You need to deploy an instance of SQL Server on Azure Virtual Machines. The solution must meet the following requirements:
• Custom performance configuration, such as IOPS, capacity, and throughout, must be supported.
• Costs must be minimized.
Which type of disk should you include in the solution?
A. Premium SSD v2
B. Premium SSD
C. Standard SSD
D. Ultra-SSD

Correct Answer: A

7. You have an on-premises datacenter that contains a 14-TB Microsoft SQL Server database.
You plan to create an Azure SQL managed instance and migrate the on-premises database to the new instance.
Which three service tiers support the SQL managed instance? Each correct answer presents a complete solution.
NOTE: Each correct selection is worth one point.
A. General Purpose Standard
B. Business Critical Memory Optimized Premium
C. General Purpose Premium
D. Business Critical Premium
E. Business Critical Standard

Correct Answer: A, B, C

8. You have a new Azure SQL database. The database contains a column that stores confidential information.
You need to track each time values from the column are returned in a query. The tracking information must be stored for 365 days from the date the query was executed.
Which three actions should you perform? Each correct answer presents part of the solution.
NOTE: Each correct selection is worth one point.
A. Turn on auditing and write audit logs to an Azure Storage account.
B. Add extended properties to the column.
C. Turn on auditing and write audit logs to an Event Hub
D. Apply sensitivity labels named Highly Confidential to the column.
E. Turn on Azure Defender for SQL

Correct Answer: A, D, E

9. You have an Azure virtual machine named VM1 on a virtual network named VNet1. Outbound traffic from VM1 to the internet is blocked.
You have an Azure SQL database named SqlDb1 on a logical server named SqlSrv1.
You need to implement connectivity between VM1 and SqlDb1 to meet the following requirements:
• Ensure that all traffic to the public endpoint of SqlSrv1 is blocked.
• Minimize the possibility of VM1 exfiltrating data stored in SqlDb1.
What should you create on VNet1?
A. a VPN gateway
B. a service endpoint
C. a private link
D. an ExpressRoute gateway

Correct Answer: C

10. DRAG DROP –
You have a new Azure SQL database named DB1 on an Azure SQL server named AzSQL1.
The only user who was created is the server administrator.
You need to create a contained database user in DB1 who will use Azure Active Directory (Azure AD) for authentication.
Which three actions should you perform in sequence? To answer, move the appropriate actions from the list of actions to the answer area and arrange them in the correct order.
Select and Place:

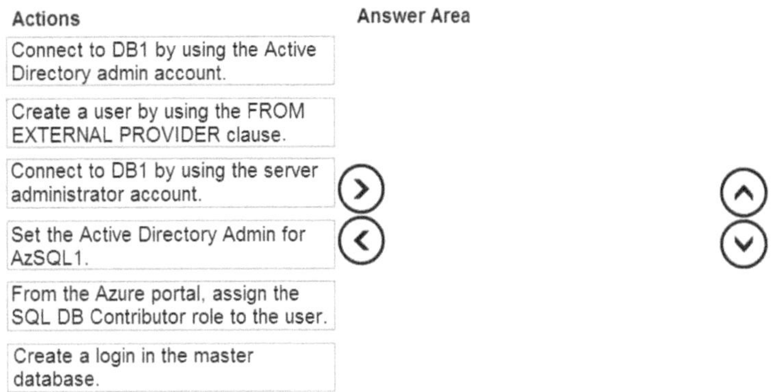

Correct Answer:

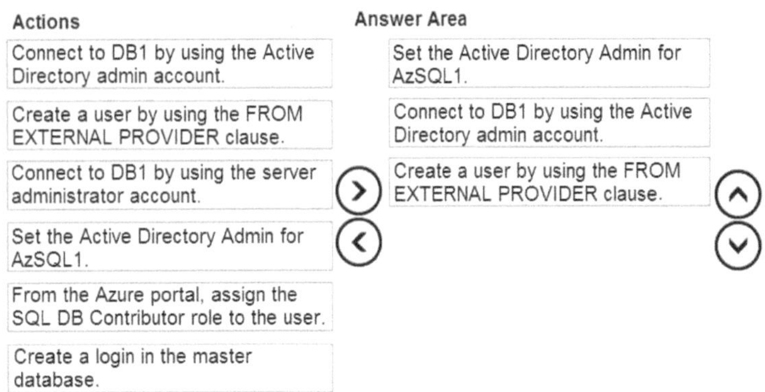

11. HOTSPOT -

You have an Azure SQL database that contains a table named Customer. Customer has the columns shown in the following table.

Customer_ID	Customer_Name	Customer_Phone
11001	Contoso, Ltd	555-555-0173
11002	Litware, Inc.	555-505-3124
11003	ADatum Corporation	555-689-4312

You plan to implement a dynamic data mask for the Customer_Phone column. The mask must meet the following requirements:

- The first six numerals of each customer's phone number must be masked.
- The last four digits of each customer's phone number must be visible.
- Hyphens must be preserved and displayed.

How should you configure the dynamic data mask? To answer, select the appropriate options in the answer area.

Hot Area:

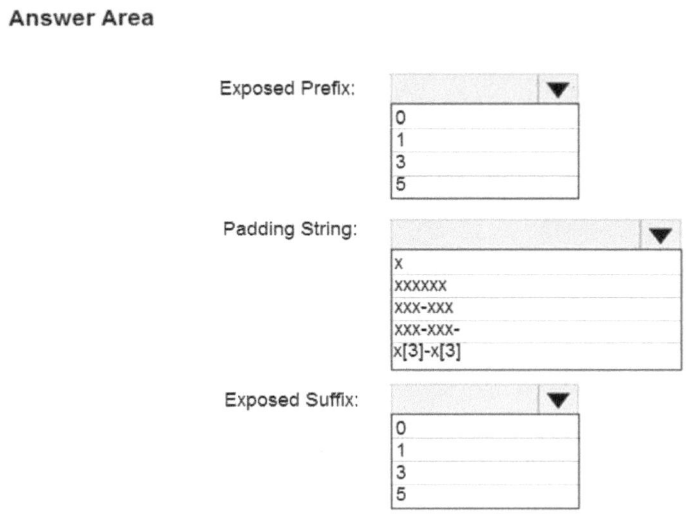

Correct Answer:

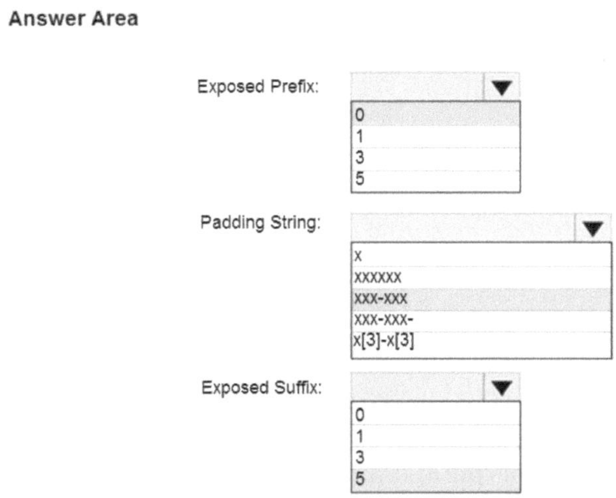

12. DRAG DROP –

You have an Azure SQL database that contains a table named Employees. Employees contains a column named Salary.

You need to encrypt the Salary column. The solution must prevent database administrators from reading the data in the Salary column and must provide the most secure encryption.

Which three actions should you perform in sequence? To answer, move the appropriate actions from the list of actions
to the answer area and arrange them in the correct order.

Select and Place:

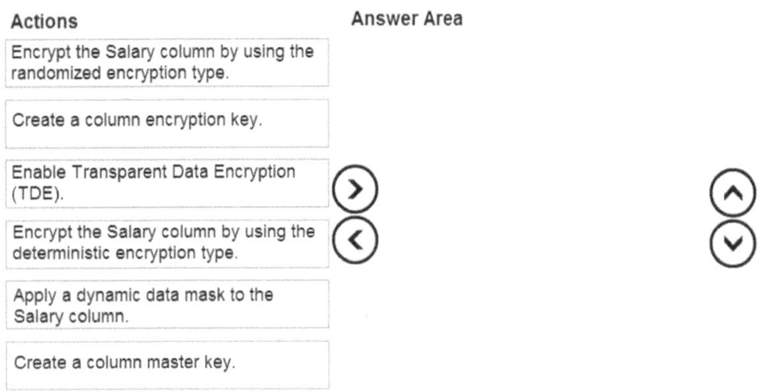

Correct Answer:

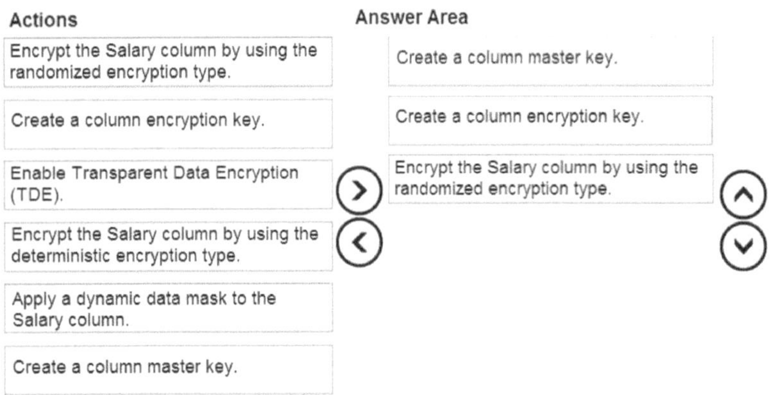

Step 1: Create a column master key
Create a column master key metadata entry before you create a column encryption key metadata entry in the database and before any column in the database can be encrypted using Always Encrypted.
Step 2: Create a column encryption key.
Step 3: Encrypt the Salary column by using the randomized encryption type.
Randomized encryption uses a method that encrypts data in a less predictable manner. Randomized encryption is more secure, but prevents searching, grouping, indexing, and joining on encrypted columns.
Note: A column encryption key metadata object contains one or two encrypted values of a column encryption key that is used to encrypt data in a column. Each value is encrypted using a column master key.

13. HOTSPOT -
You have an Azure SQL database named DB1 that contains two tables named Table1 and Table2. Both tables contain a column named a Column1. Column1 is used for joins by an application named App1.
You need to protect the contents of Column1 at rest, in transit, and in use.
How should you protect the contents of Column1? To answer, select the appropriate options in the answer area.
NOTE: Each correct selection is worth one point.
Hot Area:

Answer Area

Encryption key:

- Column encryption key
- Database encryption key
- Service master key

Encryption type:

- Deterministic
- Randomized
- Transparent Data Encryption (TDE)

Correct Answer:

Answer Area

Encryption key:

- Column encryption key
- Database encryption key
- Service master key

Encryption type:

- Deterministic
- Randomized
- Transparent Data Encryption (TDE)

14. You have 40 Azure SQL databases, each for a different customer. All the databases reside on the same Azure SQL Database server.
You need to ensure that each customer can only connect to and access their respective database.
Which two actions should you perform? Each correct answer presents part of the solution.
NOTE: Each correct selection is worth one point.
A. Implement row-level security (RLS).
B. Create users in each database.
C. Configure the database firewall.
D. Configure the server firewall.
E. Create logins in the master database.
F. Implement Always Encrypted.

Correct Answer: B, E

15. DRAG DROP -
You have an Azure SQL Database instance named DatabaseA on a server named Server1.
You plan to add a new user named App1 to DatabaseA and grant App1 db_datareader permissions. App1 will use SQL Server Authentication.

You need to create App1. The solution must ensure that App1 can be given access to other databases by using the same credentials.
Which three actions should you perform in sequence? To answer, move the appropriate actions from the list of actions to the answer area and arrange them in the correct order.
Select and Place:

Actions

- On the master database, run `CREATE LOGIN [APP1] FROM EXTERNAL PROVIDER;`
- On DatabaseA, run `CREATE USER [APP1] WITH PASSWORD = 'P@ssW0rd!';`
- On DatabaseA, run `ALTER ROLE db_datareader ADD MEMBER [App1];`
- On the master database, run `CREATE LOGIN [App1] WITH PASSWORD = 'P@aaW0rd!';`
- On DatabaseA, run `CREATE USER [App1] FROM LOGIN [App1];`

Answer Area

Correct Answer:

Actions

- On the master database, run `CREATE LOGIN [APP1] FROM EXTERNAL PROVIDER;`
- On DatabaseA, run `CREATE USER [APP1] WITH PASSWORD = 'P@ssW0rd!';`

Answer Area

- On the master database, run `CREATE LOGIN [App1] WITH PASSWORD = 'P@aaW0rd!';`
- On DatabaseA, run `CREATE USER [App1] FROM LOGIN [App1];`
- On DatabaseA, run `ALTER ROLE db_datareader ADD MEMBER [App1];`

16. You have an Azure virtual machine named VM1 on a virtual network named VNet1. Outbound traffic from VM1 to the internet is blocked.
You have an Azure SQL database named SqlDb1 on a logical server named SqlSrv1.
You need to implement connectivity between VM1 and SqlDb1 to meet the following requirements:
Ensure that VM1 cannot connect to any Azure SQL Server other than SqlSrv1.
Restrict network connectivity to SqlSrv1.
What should you create on VNet1?
A. a VPN gateway
B. a service endpoint
C. a private link
D. an ExpressRoute gateway

Correct Answer: C

17. You are developing an application that uses Azure Data Lake Storage Gen 2.

You need to recommend a solution to grant permissions to a specific application for a limited time period.
What should you include in the recommendation?
A. role assignments
B. account keys
C. shared access signatures (SAS)
D. Azure Active Directory (Azure AD) identities

Correct Answer: C

18. You are designing an enterprise data warehouse in Azure Synapse Analytics that will contain a table named Customers.
Customers will contain credit card information.
You need to recommend a solution to provide salespeople with the ability to view all the entries in Customers. The solution must prevent all the salespeople from viewing or inferring the credit card information.
What should you include in the recommendation?
A. row-level security
B. data masking
C. Always Encrypted
D. column-level security
Correct Answer: B

19. HOTSPOT -
You have an Azure subscription that is linked to a hybrid Azure Active Directory (Azure AD) tenant. The subscription contains an Azure Synapse Analytics SQL pool named Pool1.
You need to recommend an authentication solution for Pool1. The solution must support multi-factor authentication (MFA) and database-level authentication.
Which authentication solution or solutions should you include in the recommendation? To answer, select the appropriate options in the answer area.
NOTE: Each correct selection is worth one point.
Hot Area:

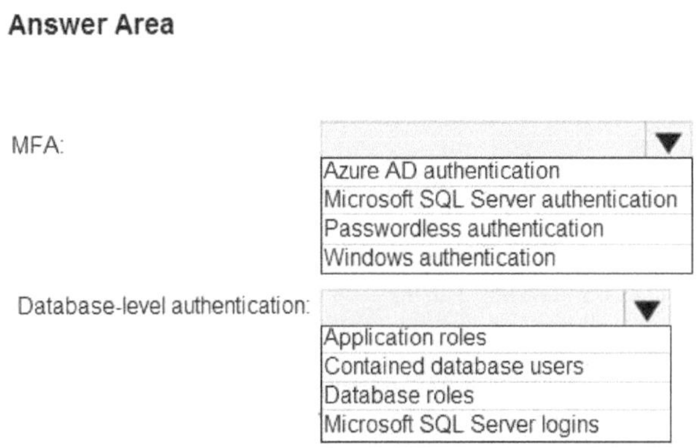

Correct Answer:

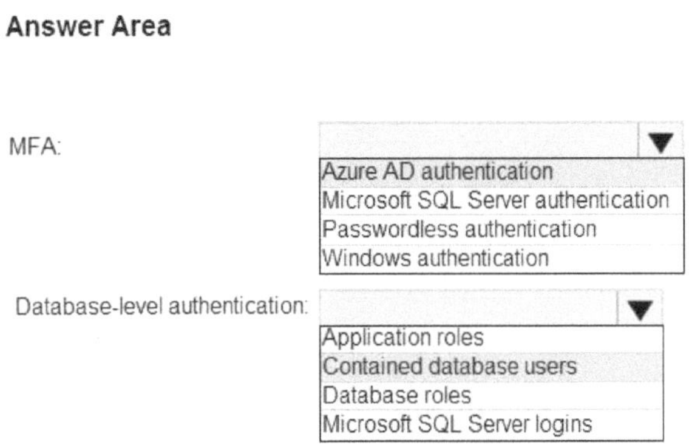

20. You have a data warehouse in Azure Synapse Analytics.
You need to ensure that the data in the data warehouse is encrypted at rest.
What should you enable?
A. Transparent Data Encryption (TDE)
B. Advanced Data Security for this database
C. Always Encrypted for all columns
D. Secure transfer required

Correct Answer: A

21. You have 20 Azure SQL databases provisioned by using the vCore purchasing model.
You plan to create an Azure SQL Database elastic pool and add the 20 databases.
Which three metrics should you use to size the elastic pool to meet the demands of your workload? Each correct answer presents part of the solution.
NOTE: Each correct selection is worth one point.
A. total size of all the databases
B. geo-replication support
C. number of concurrently peaking databases * peak CPU utilization per database
D. maximum number of concurrent sessions for all the databases
E. total number of databases * average CPU utilization per database

Correct Answer: A, C, E

22. DRAG DROP -
You have SQL Server 2019 on an Azure virtual machine that contains an SSISDB database.
A recent failure causes the master database to be lost.
You discover that all Microsoft SQL Server integration Services (SSIS) packages fail to run on the virtual machine.
Which four actions should you perform in sequence to resolve the issue? To answer, move the appropriate actions from the list of actions to the answer area and arrange them in the correct.
Select and Place:

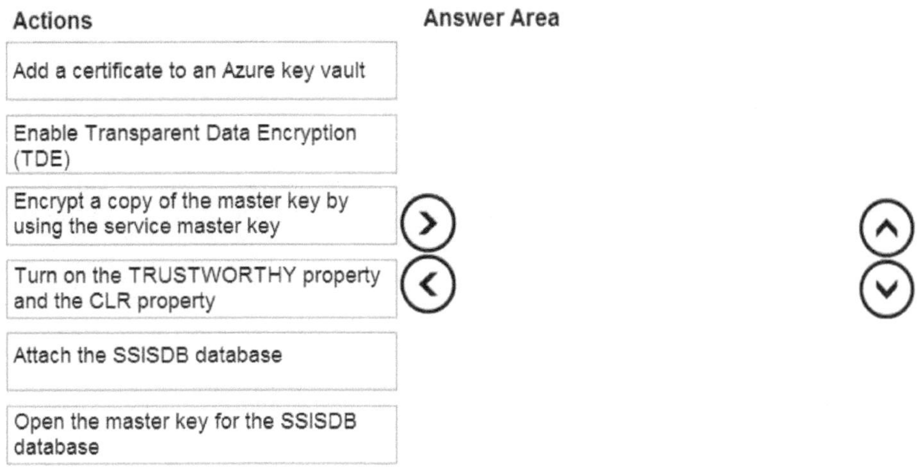

Correct Answer:

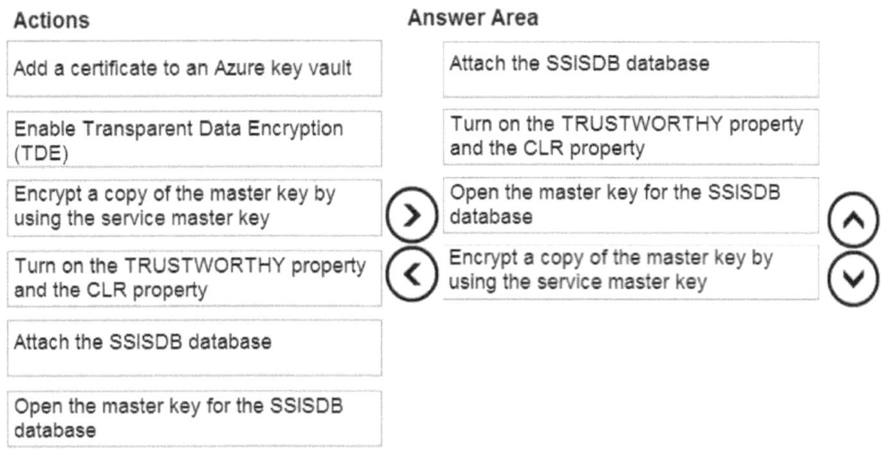

23. You have an Azure SQL database that contains a table named factSales. FactSales contains the columns shown in the following table.

Name	Data type
SalesID	Int
Product	Int
Total Number	Numeric(8,4)
Tax Number	Numeric(8,4)
SalesRep	Varchar(30)

FactSales has 6 billion rows and is loaded nightly by using a batch process. You must provide the greatest reduction in space for the database and maximize performance.
Which type of compression provides the greatest space reduction for the database?

A. page compression
B. row compression
C. columnstore compression
D. columnstore archival compression

Correct Answer: D

24. You have a Microsoft SQL Server 2019 instance in an on-premises datacentre. The instance contains a 4-TB database named DB1.
You plan to migrate DB1 to an Azure SQL Database managed instance.
What should you use to minimize downtime and data loss during the migration?
A. distributed availability groups
B. database mirroring
C. Always On Availability Group

Correct Answer: D

25. HOTSPOT -
You have an on-premises Microsoft SQL Server 2016 server named Server1 that contains a database named DB1.
You need to perform an online migration of DB1 to an Azure SQL Database managed instance by using Azure Database Migration Service.
How should you configure the backup of DB1? To answer, select the appropriate options in the answer area.
NOTE: Each correct selection is worth one point.
Hot Area:

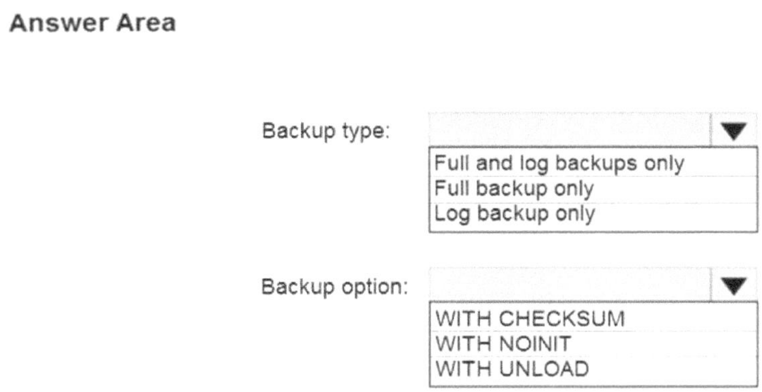

Correct Answer:

Answer Area

Backup type:

- Full and log backups only
- Full backup only
- Log backup only

Backup option:

- WITH CHECKSUM
- WITH NOINIT
- WITH UNLOAD

26. You are designing a streaming data solution that will ingest variable volumes of data.
You need to ensure that you can change the partition count after creation.
Which service should you use to ingest the data?
A. Azure Event Hubs Standard
B. Azure Stream Analytics
C. Azure Data Factory
D. Azure Event Hubs Dedicated

Correct Answer: D

27. A company is planning to deploy two Cosmos DB databases named whizlabdb1 and whizlabdb2. Below are the requirements for the databases. Costs must be minimized for both databases. The database whizlabdb1 must meet an SLA of 99.99% for both reads and writes. The database whizlabdb2 must meet an SLA of 99.99% for writes and 99.999% for reads. Which of the following would you implement for the database whizlabdb1?
A. A single read/write region
B. A single read region and multiple writes
C. A single write region and multiple reads
D. Multiple read regions and multiple write regions

Correct Answer: A

28. DRAG DROP -
You have a resource group named App1Dev that contains an Azure SQL Database server named DevServer1. DevServer1 contains an Azure SQL database named DB1. The schema and permissions for DB1 are saved in a Microsoft SQL Server Data Tools (SSDT) database project.
You need to populate a new resource group named App1Test with the DB1 database and an Azure SQL Server named TestServer1. The resources in App1Test must have the same configurations as the resources in App1Dev.
Which four actions should you perform in sequence? To answer, move the appropriate actions from the list of actions to the answer area and arrange them in the correct order.
Select and Place:

Actions

- Change the Active Directory Admin on TestServer1
- Change the server name and related variables in the templates
- From the database project, deploy the database schema and permissions
- Add IP addresses to the firewall
- From the Azure portal, export the Azure Resource Manager templates
- From the Azure portal, deploy the templates.

Answer Area

Correct Answer:

Actions

- Change the Active Directory Admin on TestServer1
- Change the server name and related variables in the templates
- From the database project, deploy the database schema and permissions
- Add IP addresses to the firewall
- From the Azure portal, export the Azure Resource Manager templates
- From the Azure portal, deploy the templates.

Answer Area

- From the Azure portal, export the Azure Resource Manager templates
- Change the server name and related variables in the templates
- From the Azure portal, deploy the templates.
- From the database project, deploy the database schema and permissions

29. HOTSPOT -

You have an Azure Synapse Analytics dedicated SQL pool named Pool1 and an Azure Data Lake Storage Gen2 account named Account1.

You plan to access the files in Account1 by using an external table.

You need to create a data source in Pool1 that you can reference when you create the external table.

How should you complete the Transact-SQL statement? To answer, select the appropriate options in the answer area.

NOTE: Each correct selection is worth one point.

Hot Area:

Answer Area

```
CREATE EXTERNAL DATA SOURCE source1
WITH
    ( LOCATION = 'https://account1.[▼].core.windows.net',
                                   blob
                                   dfs
                                   table

    [▼]
    PUSHDOWN = ON
    TYPE = BLOB_STORAGE
    TYPE = HADOOP
    )
```

Correct Answer:

Answer Area

```
CREATE EXTERNAL DATA SOURCE source1
WITH
    ( LOCATION = 'https://account1.[ ▼ ].core.windows.net',
                                    blob
                                    dfs
                                    table

    [ ▼ ]
    PUSHDOWN = ON
    TYPE = BLOB_STORAGE
    TYPE = HADOOP
    )
```

30. You have 40 Azure SQL databases, each for a different customer. All the databases reside on the same Azure SQL Database server.
You need to ensure that each customer can only connect to and access their respective database.
Which two actions should you perform? Each correct answer presents part of the solution.
NOTE: Each correct selection is worth one point.
A. Implement row-level security (RLS).
B. Create users in each database.
C. Configure the database firewall.
D. Configure the server firewall.
E. Create logins in the master database.
F. Implement Always Encrypted.

Correct Answer: B, E

31. A company is planning to deploy two Cosmos DB databases named whizlabdb1 and whizlabdb2. Below are the requirements for the databases. Costs must be minimized for both databases. The database whizlabdb1 must meet an SLA of 99.99% for both reads and writes. The database whizlabdb2 must meet an SLA of 99.99% for writes and 99.999% for reads. Which of the following would you implement for the database whizlabdb2?
A. A single read/write region
B. A single read region and multiple writes
C. A single write region and multiple reads
D. Multiple read regions and multiple write regions

Correct Answer: C

32. A company has set an Azure SQL data warehouse. They want to ensure that users use two-factor authentication when they access data from the data warehouse using SQL Server Management Studio. Which of the following would you implement for this requirement?
A. Azure AD Privileged Identity Management
B. Azure AD Identity Protection
C. Azure Key Vault

D. Azure conditional access policies

Correct Answer: D

33. A company wants to make use of Azure Databricks and Azure Data Lake Storage Gen2. As a data engineer, you have to ensure that the data in the Data Lake Storage is accessed by using a service principal from Azure Databricks. Which of the following would you implement for this requirement?
A. Use the shared access signature in Data Lake Storage.
B. Use access keys in Data Lake Storage.
C. Create an application registration in Azure AD.
D. Use a secret from Azure Key vault.

Correct Answer: C

31. DRAG DROP -
You have an Azure SQL Database instance named DatabaseA on a server named Server1.
You plan to add a new user named App1 to DatabaseA and grant App1 db_datareader permissions. App1 will use SQL Server Authentication.
You need to create App1. The solution must ensure that App1 can be given access to other databases by using the same credentials.
Which three actions should you perform in sequence? To answer, move the appropriate actions from the list of actions to the answer area and arrange them in the correct order.
Select and Place:

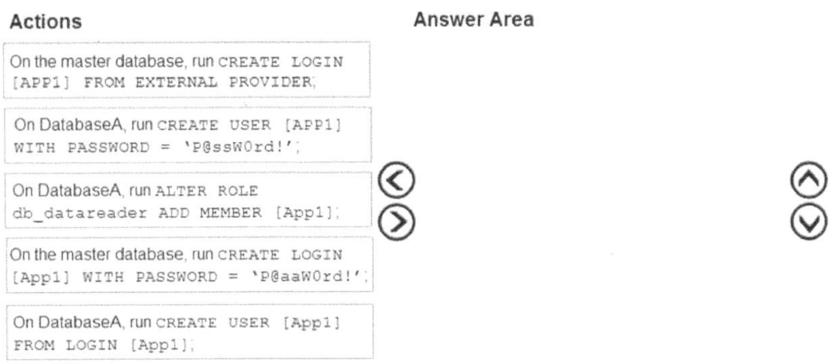

Correct Answer:

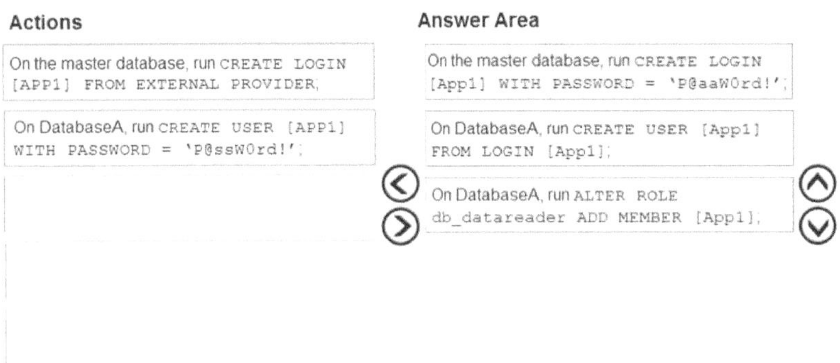

Step 1: On the master database, run CREATE LOGIN [App1] WITH PASSWORD = 'p@aaW0rd!'
Logins are server wide login and password pairs, where the login has the same password across all databases. Here is
some sample Transact-SQL that creates a login:
CREATE LOGIN readonlylogin WITH password='1231!#ASDF!a';
You must be connected to the master database on SQL Azure with the administrative login (which you get from the
SQL Azure portal) to execute the CREATE
LOGIN command.
Step 2: On DatabaseA, run CREATE USER [App1] FROM LOGIN [App1]
Users are created per database and are associated with logins. You must be connected to the database in where you
want to create the user. In most cases, this is not the master database. Here is some sample Transact-SQL that creates
a user:
CREATE USER readonlyuser FROM LOGIN readonlylogin;
Step 3: On DatabaseA run ALTER ROLE db_datareader ADD Member [App1]
Just creating the user does not give them permissions to the database. You have to grant them access. In the Transact
SQL example below the readonlyuser is given read only permissions to the database via the db_datareader role.
EXEC sp_addrolemember 'db_datareader', 'readonlyuser';

34. You have an Azure Storage Account of the kind general purpose v2. You have to grant anonymous access permission to access the blobs in a specific container only. Which of the following should you use for this requirement?
A. Access keys for the storage account
B. A shared access signature
C. Role based access control
D. Public access level for the blob service

Correct Answer: B

35. You have a Microsoft SQL Server 2019 database named DB1 that uses the following database-level and instance-level features.
• Clustered columnstore indexes
• Automatic tuning
• Change tracking
• PolyBase
You plan to migrate DB1 to an Azure SQL database.
What feature should be removed or replaced before DB1 can be migrated?
A. Clustered columnstore indexes
B. PolyBase
C. Change tracking
D. Automatic tuning

Correct Answer: B

36. You are going to create an Azure SQL data warehouse that is going to container customer data. You need to design a solution with the following requirements.
Provide the ability for data engineers to view all the rows for the customers. The data engineers should not be able to view the credit card information of the customers. Which of the following would you implement for this requirement?
A. Row-level security
B. Data masking
C. Column-level security
D. Always Encrypted

Correct Answer: B

37. You have an Azure virtual machine named VM1 on a virtual network named VNet1. Outbound traffic from VM1 to the internet is blocked.
You have an Azure SQL database named SqlDb1 on a logical server named SqlSrv1.
You need to implement connectivity between VM1 and SqlDb1 to meet the following requirements:
• Ensure that VM1 cannot connect to any Azure SQL Server other than SqlSrv1.
• Restrict network connectivity to SqlSrv1.
What should you create on VNet1?
A. a VPN gateways
B. a service endpoint
C. a private link
D. an ExpressRoute gateways

Correct Answer: C

38. A company wants to implement a big data solution on the Azure platform. The solution must meet the following requirements. Must be optimized to carry out batch processing activities. Must support autoscaling. Must support scaling at the cluster level. Which of the following would you implement for this requirement?
A. Azure Data warehouse
B. Azure HDInsight with Spark
C. Azure Analysis services
D. Azure Databricks

Correct Answer: D

39. A company has an Azure SQL Data warehouse. The company wants to have a solution in place wherein the data would be available at the time of a data center failure. The recovery point objective for the data should be an hour. Which of the following would you implement for this solution? Choose 3 Correct Answers from the options given below.
A. Restore the data warehouse from a geo-redundant backup.
B. Restore the data warehouse from a user-defined restore point.

C. Ensure that any application connection strings are updated to the recovered data warehouse.
D. Ensure to modify the Azure Firewall rules of the data warehouse.
E. Ensure to create Azure Firewall rules to allow access to the restored data warehouse.

Correct Answer: B, C and E

40. You are developing an application that uses Azure Data Lake Storage Gen 2.
You need to recommend a solution to grant permissions to a specific application for a limited time period.
What should you include in the recommendation?
A. role assignments
B. account keys
C. shared access signatures (SAS)
D. Azure Active Directory (Azure AD) identities

Correct Answer: C

41. company has an Azure Data Lake Storage Gen 2 account that is used to store data used by data engineers. The data engineers would query the data by using notebooks from Azure data bricks. The folders in the Data Lake storage account would be secured by ensuring that users only have access to the folders they require. Which of the following would you use as the authentication method for Azure Databricks?
A. Azure Active Directory
B. Azure Key vault secrets
C. Personal Access token
D. Storage access keys

Correct Answer: C

42. A company has an Azure Data Lake Storage Gen 2 account used to store data used by data engineers. The data engineers would query the data by using notebooks from Azure data bricks. The folders in the Data Lake storage account would be secured by ensuring that users only have access to the folders they require. Which of the following would you use as the authentication method for Data Lake storage?
A. Azure Active Directory
B. Shared access keys
C. Shared access signatures
D. Storage access keys

Correct Answer: A

43. You are designing an enterprise data warehouse in Azure Synapse Analytics that will contain a table named Customers. Customers will contain credit card information.
You need to recommend a solution to provide salespeople with the ability to view all the entries in Customers. The solution must prevent all the salespeople from viewing or inferring the credit card information.
What should you include in the recommendation?
A. row-level security

B. data masking
C. Always Encrypted
D. column-level security

Correct Answer: B

44. A company is planning to set up an Azure SQL database. The database will be used to store sensitive data. Below are the requirements for the data store. Only the application accessing the data can perform the encryption. The client application must have the access keys for encrypting and decrypting the data. The data must not appear in plaintext in the database. The strongest encryption method must be used on the database. The application should be able to search on select data values. Which of the following would you use as the encryption method for Searchable data?
A. Always Encrypted with randomized encryption
B. Always Encrypted with deterministic encryption
C. CREATE SYMMETRIC KEY statement.
D. CREATE CERTIFICATE statement

Correct Answer: B

45. You have a data warehouse in Azure Synapse Analytics.
You need to ensure that the data in the data warehouse is encrypted at rest.
What should you enable?
A. Transparent Data Encryption (TDE)
B. Advanced Data Security for this database
C. Always Encrypted for all columns
D. Secure transfer required

Correct Answer: A

46. A company is planning to set up an Azure SQL database. The database will be used to store sensitive data. Below are the requirements for the data store. Only the application accessing the data can perform the encryption. The client application must have the access keys for encrypting and decrypting the data. The data must not appear in plaintext in the database.
The strongest encryption method must be used on the database. The application should be able to search on select data values. Which of the following would you use as the encryption method for Non-Searchable data?
A. A.Always Encrypted with randomized encryption
B. B.Always Encrypted with deterministic encryption
C. C.CREATE SYMMETRIC KEY statement
D. D.CREATE CERTIFICATE statement

Correct Answer: A

47. A company is planning to design a solution in Azure. The solution would be based on the Lambda architecture as shown below. Which of the following service would you use for Layer 2?
A. Azure Data Lake Storage Gen 2
B. Azure Event Hubs
C. Azure Log Analytics
D. Azure SQL Data Warehouse

Correct Answer: A

48. You have a dedicated virtual machine that monitors and collects data from SQL Server instance on Azure to investigate performance issues.
The dedicated machine has the following components installed.
• Azure Monitor Agent
• Workload Insights extension
To get started with SQL Insights, from the Monitor blade, we create a profile after selecting SQL (preview).
Name the component we need to configure from "Create profile Page" that would help to send all monitoring data.
A. Monitoring profile
B. Collection settings
C. Log Analytics workspace
D. Azure Activity Log

Correct Answer: C

Chapter 2: Part 2

51. You have an Azure subscription and along with it you have a SQL Server Database which is causing a lot of performance issues.
You have set up an extended events engine in Azure SQL which is a lightweight and powerful monitoring system that allows you to capture granular information about activity in your databases and servers.
Which Channel within the Extended event is typically related to performance?
A. Admin Events
B. Operational Events
C. Analytic Events
D. Debug Events

Correct Answer: C

52. A company is planning to build a solution that would contain the below layers. You have to decide on which services will be used for each layer.

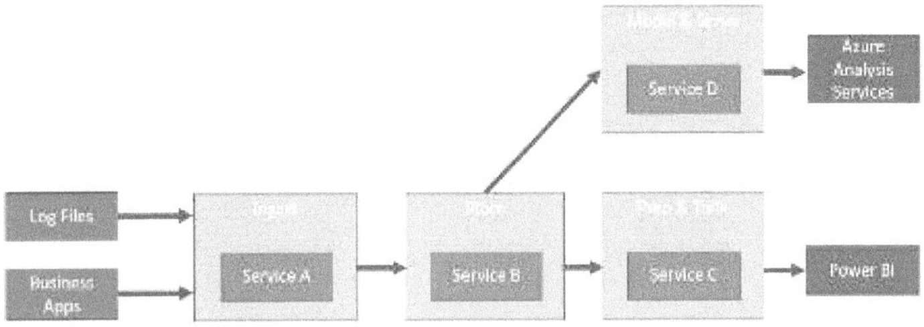

Which of the following would you choose as the service to use Service A?
A. Azure Blob Storage
B. Azure Data Factory
C. Azure Databricks
D. Azure SQL Datawarehouse

Correct Answer: B

53. You have a Microsoft Azure Subscription that holds an Azure SQL Managed Instance. This holds tables on various modules of an ERP system. You need to configure automatic tuning on the Azure SQL Managed Instance. Which Automatic tuning option is available for Instance database support?
a. FORCE_LAST_GOOD_PLAN
b. CREATE INDEX
c. DROP INDEX
d. CREATE PRIMARY KEY CONSTRAINT

Correct Answer: A

54. A company is planning to build a solution that would contain the below layers.

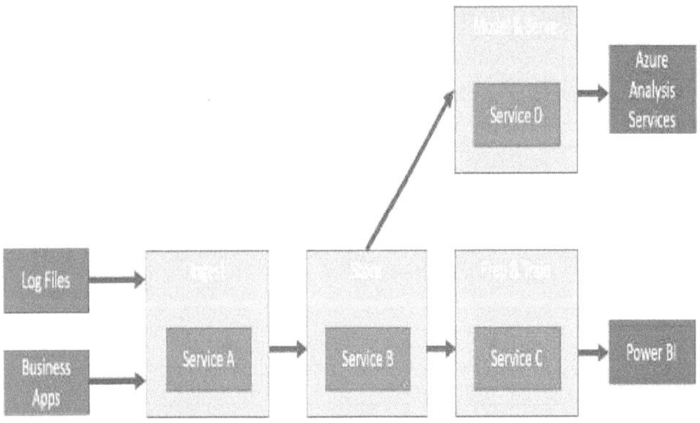

You have to decide on which services will be used for each layer. Which of the following would you choose as the service to use Service B?
A. Azure Blob Storage
B. Azure Data Factory
C. Azure Databricks
D. Azure SQL Datawarehouse

Correct Answer: A

55. You have a 'server01' running HADR with a primary role and it crashes. The DBA performs a HADR takeover by force on the 'servers02' to switch roles. The 'server02' now becomes the primary server. The below DMVs provide information on the state of a replica. Match the correct definition with their respective DMVs.

	DMV'S		ANSWER AREA
1	sys.dm_hadr_availability_replica_states	A	Returns a row for each Always On availability replica of all Always On availability groups
2	sys.dm_hadr_database_replica_states	B	Returns a row for each local replica and a row for each remote replica in the same Always On availability group
3	sys.dm_hadr_database_replica_cluster_states	C	Returns a row for each database that is participating in an Always On availability group for which the local instance of SQL Server is hosting an availability replica
4	sys.dm_hadr_availability_replica_cluster_states	D	Returns a row containing information intended to provide you with insight into the health of the available databases in the Always On availability groups in each Always On availability group on the Windows Server Failover Clustering cluster

Correct Answer: 1-B, 2-C, 3-D and 4-A

56. A company is planning to build a solution that would contain the below layers.

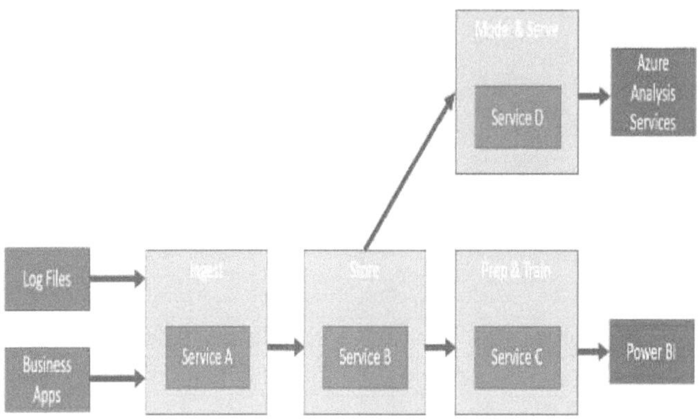

You have to decide on which services will be used for each layer. Which of the following would you choose as the service to use Service C?

A. Azure Blob Storage
B. Azure Data Factory
C. Azure Databricks
D. Azure SQL Datawarehouse

Correct Answer: C

57. You have an Azure SQL server virtual machine.

You need to back up the transaction log from the Primary server instance to the secondary server instance. Which option should you choose?
A. Implement 'Always On' availability groups
B. Configure transactional replication
C. Configure Transaction Log Shipping
D. Import a DACPAC

Correct Answer: C

58. A company is planning to build a solution that would contain the below layers.

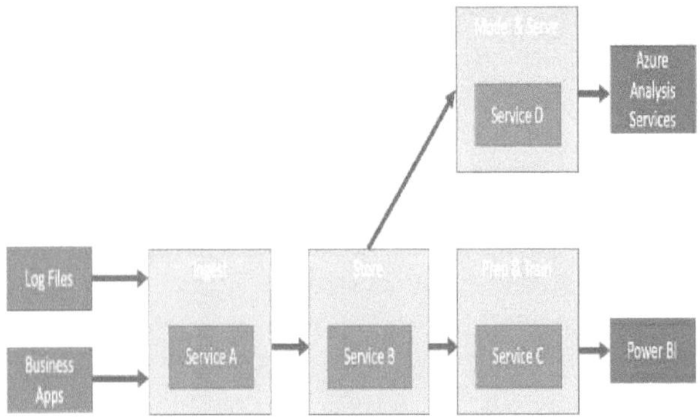

You have to decide on which services will be used for each layer. Which of the following would you choose as the service to use Service D?
A. Azure Blob Storage
B. Azure Data Factory
C. Azure Databricks
D. Azure SQL Datawarehouse

Correct Answer: D

59. A company currently stores data about its customers. The different properties of the customer data are shown below.

Name	Data populated	Unique values	Distinct values
Customer ID	100%	Each value is unique	50,000
Customer Surname	98%	50% of the values are unique	32,000
Customer Given Name	98%	50% of the values are unique	25,000
Customer Birth Date	97%	30% of the values are unique	150
Customer Category	100%	0% of the values are unique	30

The data is going to be stored in an Azure Cosmos DB container. The queries on the data will be filtered by using the Customer Category and the Customer Surname.
Which of the following would you use as the Partition Key?
A. Customer ID

B. Customer Surname
C. Customer Given Name
D. Customer Category

Correct Answer: D

60. You have a large production Azure SQL database named 'bankdb'. You are running a reporting or analytics workload on this data that is causing performance issues.
To overcome this issue you decide to have a second database such that additional workload can be handled thereby minimizing the performance impact on your production workload. Data Sync helps you to keep the two databases synchronized. Below are the steps required to set up SQL Data Sync between databases. Identify the correct sequence from the options below.
A. Add a Database in Azure SQL Database
B. Add a SQL Server Database
C. Create a Sync group
D. Configure Sync Group
E. Add Sync Member

Correct Answer: A

71. Which of the following would you use as the Item ID?
A. Customer ID
B. Customer Surname
C. Customer Given Name
D. Customer Category

Correct Answer: A

72. A company is planning on implementing an Azure data warehousing solution. A snippet of the tables in the data warehouse is shown below.

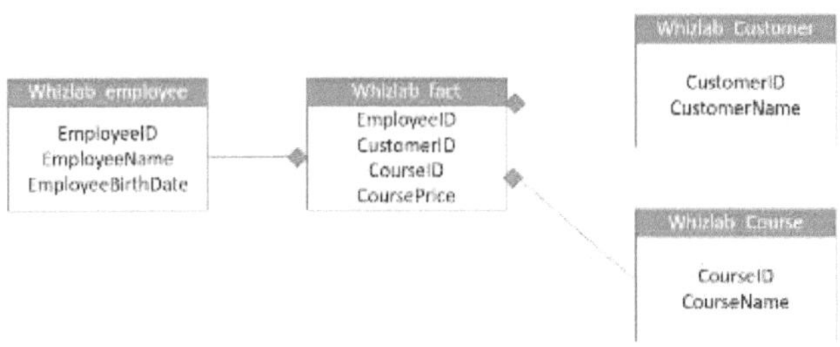

All dimension tables will be less than 4 GB after compression. The fact table will be approximately 5 TB. You have to decide on the underlying table type for each table. Which of the following would you use as the underlying table type for the Whizlab_employee table?
A. Primary
B. Hash distributed
C. Replicated
D. Round-robin

Correct Answer: C

73. You have an Azure SQL manage instance that has a database named IBC-data that stores data in geo-redundant storage blobs which are replicated to a paired region. Match the following storage redundancies for backup.

BACKUP STORAGE EDUNDANCIES		ANSWER AREA
Locally redundant storage (LRS)	A	Copying your backups synchronously three times within a single physical location in the primary region using LRS. Then it copies your data asynchronously three times to a single physical location in the paired secondary region.
Zone-redundant storage (ZRS)	B	Copies your backups synchronously across three Azure availability zones in the primary region.
Geo-redundant storage (GRS)	C	Copies your backups synchronously three times within a single physical location in the primary region

Correct Answer: 1-C, 2-B and 3-A

74. Which of the following would you use as the underlying table type for the Whizlab_fact table?
A. Primary
B. Hash distributed
C. Replicated
D. Round-robin

Correct Answer: B.

75. Which of the following would you use as the underlying table type for the Whizlab_Customer table?
A. Primary
B. Hash distributed
C. Replicated
D. Round-robin

Correct Answer: C

76. You have a Microsoft Azure SQL database instance running in the single-user mode for a POS application that manages sales and performs day to day operations of the retail store. We have a table named product_specification. The non-cluster index is created on columns batch_number, name, description, and price. There was a loss of data due to a deadlock caused when multiple users started performing CRUD operations.
Which parameter option under the DBCC(Database Console Commands) check would ensure an integrity check for the given table with no data loss?
A. NOINDEX
B. REPAIR_FAST
C. REPAIR_REBUILD
D. REPAIR_ALLOW_DATA_LOSS

Correct Answer: C

77. Which of the following would you use as the underlying table type for the Whizlab_Course table?
A. Primary
B. Hash distributed
C. Replicated
D. Round-robin

Correct Answer: C

78. An instance of Microsoft Azure SQL Server has a Sales Database with multiple objects. You have multiple indexes created on tables. Index pages are increasing massively because of the Insert and Update operation.
Name a stored procedure that provides all information about the fragmentation page and space.
A. dm_db_index_physical_stats
B. dm_db_column_store_row_group_physical_stats
C. dm_db_index_usage_stats
D. dm_db_index_operational_stats

Correct Answer: A

79. A company wants to create multiple Cosmos DB accounts. Each account has different requirements. Below are the requirements for each account. Whizlabaccount-stag – This account should be able to store log records. Whizlabaccount-prod – This account should be able to store Social media mentions. Which of the following would you use as the API for the Whizlabaccount-stag account?
A. Cassandra
B. Gremlin
C. SQL
D. Table

Correct Answer: C

80. Which of the following would you use as the API for the Whizlabaccount-prod account?
A. Cassandra
B. Gremlin
C. SQL
D. Table

Correct Answer: B

81. You need to run a Transact-SQL system stored procedure on the Microsoft Azure job agent database. For this, we need to add a new target server member to the target group containing server(s) and exclude a database target member MappingDB from the server target group. Identify the procedure that would help us perform the above tasks.
A. jobs.target_groups
B. jobs.sp_add_target_group
C. jobs.sp_add_target_group_member
D. jobs.target_group_members

Correct Answer: C

82. A company is designing an application that would be used to store images. They are going to be using Azure blob storage. They have the following requirements when it comes to the storage of images. When an image is first uploaded, it would be accessed frequently. After a week, the images would not be accessed frequently. But if accessed, it would need to be available within 30 seconds. After a year, the data would not be accessed that frequently, but it would need to be available within 5 minutes if it was accessed. The data storage costs must be minimized. Which of the following would you choose as the storage tier for the images for the first week?

A. Hot
B. Cool
C. Stale
D. Archive

Correct Answer: A

83. A company is designing an application that would be used to store images. They are going to be using Azure blob storage. They have the following requirements when it comes to the storage of images. When an image is first uploaded, it would be accessed frequently. After a week, the images would not be accessed frequently. But if accessed, it would need to be available within 30 seconds. After a year, the data would not be accessed that frequently, but it would need to be available within 5 minutes if it was accessed. The data storage costs must be minimized. Which of the following would you choose as the storage tier for the images after a month?

A. Hot
B. Cool
C. Stale
D. Archive.

Correct Answer: B

84. We have a SQL Server on an Azure VM named CHC-DB-SERVER which holds databases such as RV Medicare, and Medicaid for various clients of an insurance claim company. You add a user as a member of the sysadmin group who would be the SQL Agent operator such that it receives emails as an alert on every job failure. You need to perform certain actions from the below options to achieve the requirement.

A. Create a Job Alert
B. Enable Database Mail
C. Create a Job Notification
D. Enable Email setting for SQL Server Agent
E. Create a targeted Job

Correct Answers: B, D and E

85. A company is designing an application that would be used to store images. They are going to be using Azure blob storage. They have the following requirements when it comes to the storage of images. When an image is first uploaded it would be accessed frequently. After a week, the images would not be accessed frequently. But if accessed, it would need to be available within 30 seconds. After a year the data would not be accessed that frequently, but if it was accessed, it would need to be available within 5 minutes. The data storage costs must be minimized. Which of the following would you choose as the storage tier for the images after a year?
A. Hot
B. Cool
C. Stale
D. Archive

Correct Answer: D

86. You have a Microsoft Azure SQL server virtual machine. You wish to install log shipping such that you could store backups on a dedicated SMTP file share. You need to configure servers to perform the Log Shipping step. Which server instance would you choose to configure and perform actions such as complete backup job & copy backup Job You can choose the same server instance for different actions performed.
A. Monitor Server Instance
B. Primary Server Instance
C. Secondary Server Instance
D. Backup Share file Server

Correct Answers: B and C

87. Your company wants to design a system that would consist of an Azure virtual machine and an Azure SQL database. The database would not have any Internet connectivity. You need to implement a solution that would ensure that the virtual machine could access the database. Which of the following would you implement for this requirement?
A. Add a virtual network service endpoint.
B. Add an Application gateway.
C. Add a virtual network gateway.
D. Add an Azure Load balancer.

Correct Answer: A

88. A company wants to design a data store that would be used to store telemetry data. Which of the following could be used as the underlying data store?
A. Azure Databricks
B. Azure SQL data warehouse
C. Azure Cosmos DB
D. Azure Functions.

Correct Answer: C

89. I want to compress my table dbo.myTable. I start with the following code:
• ALTER TABLE dbo.myTable
• REBUILD PARTITION = ALL
• WITH (DATA_COMPRESSION =
Which of the options is NOT a valid ending to this code?
A. PAGE)
B. ROW)
C. NONE)
D. PREFIX)

Correct Answer: D

90. Your company is planning to use the Azure SQL database and Azure storage accounts for an application. The application would extract data, convert the data to text documents and store them in the storage account. The text documents must be accessible from an SMB network share. Which of the following would you use as the underlying service type for the Azure storage account?
A. Queue
B. Files
C. Blob
D. Table

Correct Answer: B

91. A company has an on-premise Microsoft SQL Server. They want to migrate the database to Azure SQL Databases. Which of the following would they use as the file type for exporting the on-premise database?
A. BACPAC
B. DAC
C. VHD
D. VHDX

Correct Answer: A

92. You plan to create a table in an Azure Synapse Analytics dedicated SQL pool. The data in the table is invoice data under the sales schema for the past 3 years. SQL Monitor has raised a “Long running query” which when executed showed details about all invoices generated over years to gather month-wise sales for individual items. Due to this management decided to purge data, once a year for data that is older than three years.
Using which of the options below can you ensure that data can be distributed evenly across partitions such that the operation of purging data is accelerated?
A. Filegroup
B. Partition scheme
C. Partition Function
D. Partition Column

Correct Answer: C

93. A company has an on-premise Microsoft SQL Server. They want to migrate the database to Azure SQL Databases. Which of the following should be the underlying storage type for the exported data?
A. Blob
B. Disk
C. File
D. Queue

Correct Answer: A

94. Your company currently stores data in different types of Azure cloud-based databases. The company wants to consolidate the data into a single relational database. The data would be ingested at a set time of the day. Which of the following could be a recommendation to implement this requirement?
A. SQL Server Migration Assistant
B. SQL Data Sync
C. Azure Data Factory
D. Azure Database Migration Service

Correct Answer: C

95. You plan to create a table and you need to establish trust around the integrity of data stored. Ledger provides a chronicle of all alternates made to the database over time. Choose the right option that best defines the ledger table.
A. Implements Row level security
B. Implements Encryption of data.
C. Implements decryption of data
D. Preserves historical data in the history table.

Correct Answer: D

96. A company wants to implement an Azure Databricks cluster. The cluster configuration needs to meet the following requirements. Multiple users must be able to use the cluster. Overall costs must be reduced. Query latency should be minimized. Which of the following should be implemented as the cluster configuration for this requirement?
A. Standard cluster with Autoscaling enabled
B. High Concurrency cluster with Autoscaling enabled
C. Standard cluster with Auto Termination enabled
D. High Concurrency cluster with Auto Termination enabled

Correct Answer: B

97. A company wants to migrate an on-premise MySQL database that is 800 GB in size. The database needs to be migrated to Azure database for MySQL. The migration must be performed in such a way that it would minimize interruptions to applications that use the database. Which of the following would you use to fulfill this requirement?

A. Azure Database Migration Service
B. Import and Export
C. Azure Data Sync
D. MySQL WorkBench

Correct Answer: A

98. London Heathrow Airport is one of the busiest in Europe by passenger traffic. To keep adverse weather, aircraft delays, traffic-clogged highways, public transport slow-downs, and global pandemics from disrupting its operational readiness, and to identify the untapped capacity that it can use to grow sustainably, Heathrow needs an effectively managed data estate. Which Microsoft Azure service would help derive data-driven insights to optimize its operations, support continued growth, and improve air travel experiences.
A. Data Catalog
B. Microsoft Purview
C. Azure Lighthouse
D. Azure CycleCloud

Correct Answer: B

99. A company wants to use the Azure SQL database service. Business apps will be accessing the database. They want to create an Azure SQL database managed instance. They want to ensure that the database can automatically recover from a full or partial loss of the Azure SQL database service in the primary region. Which of the following can help achieve this requirement?
A. Failover-groups
B. Azure SQL Data Sync
C. SQL Replication
D. Active geo-replication

Correct Answer: A

100. A company is making use of Azure stream analytics for a solution. They want to ensure that the solution remains available even in the event of Azure service updates. Which of the following should they implement for this requirement? Choose 2 Correct Answers from the options given below.
A. Deploy an Azure Stream Analytics job to one region that is part of a paired region.
B. Deploy an Azure Stream Analytics job to each region of a paired region.
C. Monitor jobs in both regions for failure.
D. Monitor the job in the primary region for failure.

Correct Answer: B, C

Chapter 3: Part 3

101. A company needs to design a solution that would require to perform analytics and visualization on a large data set. The solution should use notebooks, automate clusters and provide the ability to use Power BI to visualize the data. Which of the following would you use for this requirement?
A. Azure Batch
B. Azure Stream Analytics
C. Azure Databricks
D. Azure HDInsight

Correct Answer: C

102. We have an Azure SQL Database server named IBC_010122 that stores PHI data for customers at Change health care. This data is accessed and transmitted across networks between the database Server and various HealthTech, and InsurTech Client applications. To encrypt data that is transmitted across networks which form of data encryption is most suitable?
A. Always Encrypted
B. TLS
C. TDE
D. CLE

Correct Answer: B

103. You want to make use of Azure Stream Analytics. The Stream Analytics instance will be receiving data from IoT enabled devices. You need to send the data onto Cosmos DB. Which of the following would you need to set in Azure Stream Analytics?
A. A container input target.
B. A Cosmos DB input target
C. A container output target
D. A Cosmos DB output target

Correct Answer: D

104. You need to migrate a disk-based table for sales data on a SQL 2014 server to SQL 2016 such that we could have these tables as memory-optimized. A back and restore option was used for this operation. The need for this migration was to improve performance. Determine the Transact-SQL segments you should use such that the performance benefits are concluded and table statistics are updated consequently.

	SQL SEGMENTS
A	Create procedure sp_inventory WITH NATIVE COMPILATION
B	ALTER DATABASE CURRENT SET COMPATIBILITY_LEVEL = 130
C	EXEC sp_inventory
D	UPDATE STATISTICS dbo.sales
E	EXEC sp_recompile N' sp_inventory

Correct Answers: B, D and E

105. You want to make use of Azure Stream Analytics. The Stream Analytics instance will be receiving data from IoT enabled devices. You need to send the data to Cosmos DB. Which of the following needs to be created in Cosmos DB beforehand?
A. A container
B. A document store
C. A file store
D. A table

Correct Answer: A

106. A company wants to design a data processing system. Data would be ingested via Kafta streams into Azure Data Lake Storage. The data needs to be processed by an Apache Spark-based analytics service. The company decides to use Azure SQL Data Warehouse as the analytics service. Would this fulfill the requirement?
A. Yes
B. No

Correct Answer: B

107. A company holds a Microsoft cloud subscription. We need to understand how we enable the staff of the company to connect to the cloud services.
We have the Azure virtual network gateway to access the cloud environment.
To ensure a secure connection for all of the users who work at the office, between the data center or office and the Azure virtual network, which of the following VPN option would you choose from below?
A. site to site (S2S) VPN
B. IPSec
C. ExpressRoute
D. point-to-site VPN

Correct Answer: A

108. A company wants to design a data processing system. Data would be ingested via Kafta streams into Azure Data Lake Storage. The data needs to be processed by an Apache Spark-based analytics service. The company decides to use Azure Databricks as the analytics service. Would this fulfill the requirement?
A. Yes
B. No

Correct Answer: A

109. A company wants to design a data processing system. Data would be ingested via Kafta streams into Azure Data Lake Storage. The data needs to be processed by an Apache Spark-based analytics service.

The company decides to use Azure Stream Analytics as the analytics service. Would this fulfill the requirement?
A. Yes
B. No

Correct Answer: B

110. You have Customer PHI data residing at TIBCO which is a legacy service used to integrate applications using a visual, model-driven development environment by CHC. We need to migrate this data to Azure SQL Database such that we can perform certain analyses.
The TIBCO system produces time series analysis-based reports for customers who are segregated on the basis of aliment diagnosed. There are six ailments on which these analyses would broadly be carried out.
Data from the TIBCO system is stored in Azure Event Hub.
For being affirmative on the diagnosis done for the aliment the reports would be sent to four other departments such that pre-operative assessment and examination tests could be carried out.
Each department has an Azure Web App that displays time series-based assessment and contains a WebJob that processes incoming data from Event Hub.
All Web Apps run on App Service Plans with three instances.
Data throughput must be maximized. Latency must be minimized.
You need to implement the Azure Event Hub. The partition Key is ‘department’. What would be the number of partitions required for optimal data distribution?
A. 3
B. 4
C. 6
D. 12

Correct Answer: C

111. A company wants to design a data processing system. Data would be ingested via Kafta streams into Azure Data Lake Storage. The data needs to be processed by an Apache Spark-based analytics service. The company decides to use Azure Analysis service as the analytics service. Would this fulfill the requirement?
A. Yes
B. No

Correct Answer: B

112. A company wants to deploy a Cosmos DB account. The data within the account will be used by data engineers situated across the world. You need to ensure that data engineers worldwide can access the data for a read operation with the least amount of latency. You also need to ensure that costs are minimized. Which of the following would you implement for this requirement?
A. Create a single Azure Cosmos DB account and enable multi-region writes.
B. Create a single Azure Cosmos DB account and configure data replication.
C. Create a single Azure Cosmos DB account and configure geo-redundancy.
D. Create multiple Azure Cosmos DB accounts for each region.

Correct Answer: B

113. You have an Azure Data Lake Storage Gen 2 account. You have to grant permissions to a specific application for a limited time period. Which of the following can you use for this requirement?
A. Access keys for the storage account
B. A shared access signature
C. Role based access control
D. Azure AD Users

Correct Answer: B

114. What should you use to migrate the PostgreSQL database?
A. Azure Data Box
B. AzCopy
C. Azure Database Migration Service
D. Azure Site Recovery

Correct Answer: C

115. A company is planning to set an Azure SQL Database. The database contains tables and columns that contain sensitive data. The company wants to have a solution in place that would accomplish the following requirements. Ensure the database is encrypted at rest.
Ensure that when sensitive data is accessed from the columns, it is encrypted in transit. Which of the following would you use for the following requirement? "Ensure the database is encrypted at rest."
A. Always Encrypted
B. Dynamic data masking
C. Row-level security
D. Transparent Data Encryption

Correct Answer: D

116. You plan to move two 100-GB databases to Azure.
You need to dynamically scale resources consumption based on workloads. The solution must minimize downtime during scaling operations.
What should you use?
A. An Azure SQL Database elastic pool
B. SQL Server on Azure virtual machines
C. an Azure SQL Database managed instance
D. Azure SQL databases

Correct Answer: A

117. A company is planning to set an Azure SQL Database. The database contains tables and columns that contain sensitive data. The company wants to have a solution in place that would accomplish the following requirements. Ensure the database is encrypted at rest. Ensure that when sensitive data is accessed from the columns, it is encrypted in transit. Which of the following would you use for the

following requirement? “Ensure that when sensitive data is accessed from the columns, it is encrypted in transit.”
A. Always Encrypted
B. Dynamic data masking
C. Row-level security
D. Transparent Data Encryption

Correct Answer: A

118. You have 10 Azure virtual machines that have SQL Server installed.
You need to implement a backup strategy to ensure that you can restore specific databases to other SQL Server instances. The solution must provide centralized management of the backups.
What should you include in the backup strategy?
A. Automated Backup in the SQL virtual machine settings
B. Azure Backup
C. Azure Site Recovery
D. SQL Server Agent jobs

Correct Answer: B

119. You have an Azure SQL database. You need to provide an Azure AD group read access to the database. Which of the following would you use to provide access?
A. A contained database user
B. Role based access control
C. Access keys
D. Shared Access Signature

Correct Answer: A

120. You need to design a solution that would use Azure Functions. The function would be used to process data that is uploaded to Azure Blob storage. You have to ensure that the following requirements are met. The solution must have support for 1 million blobs. The solution must scale automatically. Costs must be minimized. Which of the following would you recommend for this requirement?
A. Deploying the Azure Function as part of an App Service Plan and then using the Blob trigger
B. Deploying the Azure Function as part of an App Service Plan and then using the Event trigger]
C. Deploying the Azure Function as part of a Consumption Plan and then using the Blob trigger
D. Deploying the Azure Function as part of a Consumption Plan and then using the Event trigger

Correct Answer: C

121. You need to recommend an availability strategy for an Azure SQL database. The strategy must meet the following requirements:
-Support failovers that do not require client applications to change their connection strings.
-Replicate the database to a secondary Azure region.
-Support failover to the secondary region.
What should you include in the recommendation?

A. failover groups
B. transactional replication
C. Availability Zones
D. geo-replication

Correct Answer: A

122. A company wants to design a solution that would support the ingestion and analysis of log files in real-time. Which of the following would you implement for this requirement? Choose 2 Correct Answers from the options given below.
A. Azure Databricks
B. Azure Data Factory
C. Azure Event Hubs
D. Azure Data Lake Gen 2 storage

Correct Answer: A and C

123. A company is planning to design a solution in Azure. The solution would be based on the Kappa architecture as shown below.

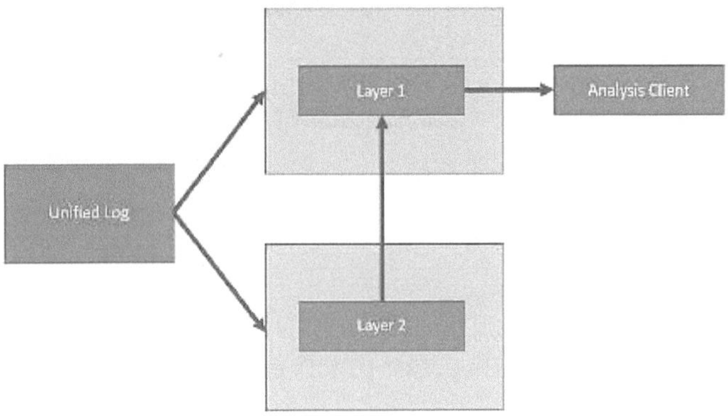

ss

Which of the following could be used for Layer 1?
A. Azure Cosmos DB
B. Azure Data Catalog
C. Azure Data Factory
D. Azure SQL Data Warehouse

Correct Answer: A

124. You are building a database backup solution for a SQL Server database hosted on an Azure virtual machine.
In the event of an Azure regional outage, you need to be able to restore the database backups. The solution must minimize costs.
Which type of storage accounts should you use for the backups?
A. locally-redundant storage (LRS)

B. read-access geo-redundant storage (RA-GRS)
C. zone-redundant storage (ZRS)
D. geo-redundant storage

Correct Answer: B

125. You have SQL Server on Azure virtual machines in an availability group. You have a database named DB1 that is NOT in the availability group. You create a full database backup of DB1.
You need to add DB1 to the availability group.
Which restore option should you use on the secondary replica?
A. Restore with Recovery
B. Restore with Norecovery
C. Restore with Standby

Correct Answer: B

126. You are planning disaster recovery for the failover group of an Azure SQL Database managed instance.
Your company's SLA requires that the database in the failover group become available as quickly as possible if a major outage occurs.
You set the Read/Write failover policy to Automatic.
What are two results of the configuration? Each correct answer presents a complete solution.
NOTE: Each correct selection is worth one point.
A. In the event of a datacenter or Azure regional outage, the databases will fail over automatically.
B. In the event of an outage, the databases in the primary instance will fail over immediately.
C. In the event of an outage, you can selectively fail over individual databases.
D. In the event of an outage, you can set a different grace period to fail over each database.
E. In the event of an outage, the minimum delay for the databases to fail over in the primary instance will be one hour.

Correct Answer: A, E

127. A company is planning to design a solution in Azure. The solution would be based on the Kappa architecture as shown below.

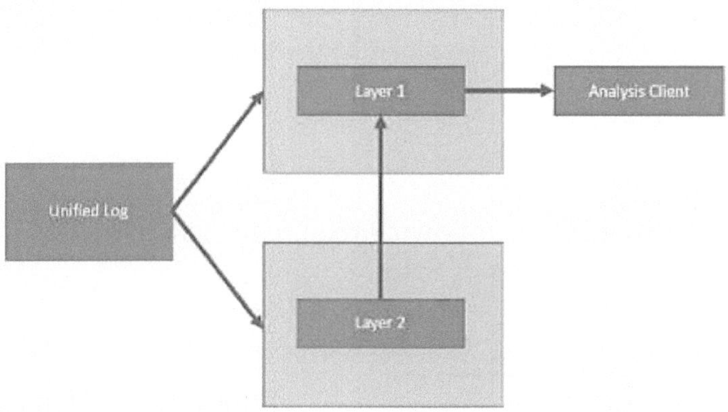

Which of the following could be used for Layer 1?
A. Azure Cosmos DB
B. Azure Data Catalog
C. Azure Data Factory
D. Azure SQL Data Warehouse

Correct Answer: D

128. A company wants to make use of an Azure Databricks interactive cluster. The cluster would be configured for auto-termination. The company wants to ensure that the cluster configuration remains indefinitely after the cluster is terminated. The company also wants to ensure that costs are minimized when implementing the solution. Which of the following would you implement for this requirement?
A. Ensure to clone the cluster.
B. Ensure to create an Azure runbook to start the cluster.
C. Ensure to pin the cluster.
D. Ensure to disable termination for the cluster.

Correct Answer: C

129. You have an Azure SQL database named DB1.
You need to ensure that DB1 will support automatic failover without data loss if a datacenter fails. The solution must minimize costs.
Which deployment option and pricing tier should you configure?
A. Azure SQL Database Premium
B. Azure SQL Database serverless
C. Azure SQL Database managed instance Business Critical
D. Azure SQL Database Standard

Correct Answer: A

130. A company wants to use an Azure Data Lake Storage account to store CSV files. These files will be organized into department wise folders. The company wants to ensure that data is configured in such a way that users will only see files in their respective department folders. They decide to disable hierarchical namespace and use access control lists. Would this fulfill the requirement?
A. Yes
B. No

Correct Answer: B

131. You have an Azure SQL database named Sales.
You need to implement disaster recovery for Sales to meet the following requirements:
-During normal operations, provide at least two readable copies of Sales.
-Ensure that Sales remains available if a datacenter fails.
Solution: You deploy an Azure SQL database that uses the General Purpose service tier and geo-replication.

Does this meet the goal?
A. Yes
B. No

Correct Answer: B

132. A company wants to use an Azure Data Lake Storage account to store CSV files. These files will be organized into department wise folders. The company wants to ensure that data is configured in such a way that users will only see files in their respective department folders. They decide to enable hierarchical namespace and use RBAC. Would this fulfill the requirement?
A. Yes
B. No

Correct Answer: B

133. A company wants to use an Azure Data Lake Storage account to store CSV files. These files will be organized into department wise folders. The company wants to ensure that data is configured in such a way that users will only see files in their respective department folders. They decide to disable the hierarchical namespace and use RBAC. Would this fulfill the requirement?
A. Yes
B. No

Correct Answer: B

134. You have an Azure SQL database named Sales.
You need to implement disaster recovery for Sales to meet the following requirements:
-During normal operations, provide at least two readable copies of Sales.
-Ensure that Sales remains available if a datacenter fails.
Solution: You deploy an Azure SQL database that uses the Business-Critical service tier and Availability Zones.
Does this meet the goal?
A. Yes
B. No

Correct Answer: A

135. A company wants to implement a big data store. Below are the key requirements for the data store. It should have support for a hierarchical file system. It should be optimized for parallel analytic workloads. It should provide unlimited account sizes. Which of the following would you implement for this requirement?
A. Azure Data Lake Storage Gen2
B. Azure Blob storage
C. Apache HBase in Azure HDInsight
D. Azure Cosmos DB

Correct Answer: A

136. You have an Azure SQL database named Sales.
You need to implement disaster recovery for Sales to meet the following requirements:
-During normal operations, provide at least two readable copies of Sales.
-Ensure that Sales remains available if a datacenter fails.
Solution: You deploy an Azure SQL database that uses the General-Purpose service tier and failover groups. Does this meet the goal?
A. Yes
B. No

Correct Answer: A

137. A company wants to implement an Azure Cosmos DB database that would support data storage for vertices and edges. Which of the following would you use as the underlying Cosmos DB API?
A. SQL
B. Cassandra
C. Gremlin
D. Table

Correct Answer: C

138. A company wants to implement a data store that would meet the following requirements. Be able to receive thousands of files per minute. The files would be in different file formats – JSON, text and CSV. The files would eventually be processed, transformed and loaded into an Azure SQL data warehouse. Which of the following would you use as the underlying data store?
A. Azure Data Lake Storage Gen2
B. Azure Blob storage
C. Apache HBase in Azure HDInsight
D. Azure Cosmos DB

Correct Answer: A

139. A company wants to migrate data from an on-premise Mongo DB Instance to Azure Cosmos DB – Mongo API. During the testing phase, they discovered that too much time is being taken for the migration process. Which of the following can they implement to reduce the migration time? Choose 2 Correct Answers from the options given below.
A. Increase the number of Request Units.
B. Look to turn off indexing.
C. Add an additional write region to the Cosmos DB account.
D. Go ahead and create unique indexes.

Correct Answer: A, B

140. You plan to move two 100-GB databases to Azure.

You need to dynamically scale resources consumption based on workloads. The solution must minimize downtime during scaling operations.
What should you use?
A. two Azure SQL Databases in an elastic pool
B. two databases hosted in SQL Server on an Azure virtual machine
C. two databases in an Azure SQL Managed instance
D. two single Azure SQL databases

Correct Answer: A

141. A company wants to deploy a set of databases using the Azure SQL database service. They want to organize the databases into separate groups based on database usage. They also want to have the ability to define the maximum limit on the resources that would be able for each group. Which of the following could be recommended to fulfill this requirement?
A. Azure SQL Database Hyperscale
B. Azure SQL Database Single Instance
C. Azure SQL Database Elastic Pools
D. Azure SQL Database Sharding

Correct Answer: C

142. A company wants to create an Azure storage account. Below are the requirements for the objects in the storage account. Storage costs should be minimized.
The storage account will be used to hold objects which are infrequently accessed. The data in the storage account will be stored for at least 30 days. Data availability must be guaranteed at an SLA of 99% Which of the following could be used as the underlying storage tier?
A. Premium
B. Hot
C. Cold
D. Archive

Correct Answer: C

143. You have an on-premises app named App1 that stores data in an on-premises Microsoft SQL Server 2016 database named DB1.
You plan to deploy additional instances of App1 to separate Azure regions. Each region will have a separate instance of App1 and DB1. The separate instances of DB1 will sync by using Azure SQL Data Sync.
You need to recommend a database service for the deployment. The solution must minimize administrative effort.
What should you include in the recommendation?
A. Azure SQL Managed instance
B. Azure SQL Database single database
C. Azure Database for PostgreSQL
D. SQL Server on Azure virtual machines

Correct Answer: B

144. You have two Azure SQL Database servers named Server1 and Server2. Each server contains an Azure SQL database named Database1.
You need to restore Database1 from Server1 to Server2. The solution must replace the existing Database1 on Server2.
Solution: From Microsoft SQL Server Management Studio (SSMS), you rename Database1 on Server2 as Database2. From the Azure portal, you create a new database on Server2 by restoring the backup of Database1 from Server1, and then you delete Database2.
Does this meet the goal?
A. Yes
B. No

Correct Answer: A

145. You have an Azure subscription that uses a domain named contoso.com.
You have two Azure VMs named DBServer1 and DBServer2. Each of them hosts a default SQL Server instance. DBServer1 is in the East US Azure region and contains a database named DatabaseA. DBServer2 is in the West US Azure region.
DBServer1 has a high volume of data changes and low latency requirements for data writes.
You need to configure a new availability group for DatabaseA. The secondary replica will reside on DBServer2. What should you do?
A. Configure the primary endpoint as TCP://DBServer1.contoso.com:445, configure the secondary endpoint as TCP://DBServer2.contoso.com:445, and set the availability mode to Asynchronous.
B. Configure the primary endpoint as TCP://DBServer1.contoso.com:445, configure the secondary endpoint as TCP://DBServer2.contoso.com:445, and set the availability mode to Synchronous.
C. Configure the primary endpoint as TCP://DBServer1.contoso.com:5022, configure the secondary endpoint as TCP://DBServer2.contoso.com:5022, and set the availability mode to Asynchronous.
D. Configure the primary endpoint as TCP://DBServer1.contoso.com:5022, configure the secondary endpoint as TCP://DBServer2.contoso.com:5022, and set the availability mode to Synchronous.

Correct Answer: C

146. You have an on-premises multi-tier application named App1 that includes a web tier, an application tier, and a Microsoft SQL Server tier. All the tiers run on Hyper-V virtual machines.
Your new disaster recovery plan requires that all business-critical applications can be recovered to Azure.
You need to recommend a solution to fail over the database tier of App1 to Azure. The solution must provide the ability to test failover to Azure without affecting the current environment.
What should you include in the recommendation?
A. Azure Backup
B. Azure Information Protection
C. Windows Server Failover Cluster
D. Azure Site Recovery

Correct Answer: D

147. A company wants to start using the Azure Databricks service. They want to ensure that the Databricks clusters remain available even at the time of regional Azure datacenter outages. Which of the following could be used as the redundancy type to fulfill this requirement?
A. Read-access geo-redundant storage
B. Locally redundant storage
C. Geo-redundant storage
D. Zone-redundant storage

Correct Answer: C

148. HOTSPOT (Drag and Drop is not supported)
You plan to migrate on-premises Microsoft SQL Server databases to Azure.
You need to identify which deployment and resiliency options meet the following requirements:
-Support user-initiated backups.
-Support multiple automatically replicated instances across Azure regions.
-Minimize administrative effort to implement and maintain business continuity.
What should you identify? To answer, select the appropriate options in the answer area.
NOTE: Each correct selection is worth one point.
Hot Area:

Answer Area

Deployment option:

▼
Azure SQL Managed Instance
SQL Server on Azure Virtual Machines
An Azure SQL Database single database

Resiliency option:

▼
Auto-failover group
Active geo-replication
Zone-redundant deployment

A. See Explanation section for answer.
Correct Answer: A
Explanation:

Deployment option:

	▼
Azure SQL Managed Instance	
SQL Server on Azure Virtual Machines	
An Azure SQL Database single database	

Resiliency option:

	▼
Auto-failover group	
Active geo-replication	
Zone-redundant deployment	

149. A company wants to use the Azure SQL database service. Business apps will be accessing the database. The application data must be available in the event of a region-wide outage. Below are the other key requirements. Data must be available in the secondary region if the primary region goes down. The storage and compute layers for the SQL database must be integrated and replicated together. Which of the following would you use as the Service tier for the database?

A. Basic
B. Standard
C. Premium
D. High

Correct Answer: C

150. A company wants to use the Azure SQL database service. Business apps will be accessing the database. The application data must be available in the event of a region-wide outage. Below are the other key requirements. Data must be available in the secondary region if the primary region goes down.
The storage and compute layers for the SQL database must be integrated and replicated together. Which of the following would you use as the redundancy type?

A. SQL Sync
B. Zone-Redundancy
C. Geo-redundant storage
D. Local-redundant storage

Correct Answer: C

151. A company is planning to use the Azure SQL data warehouse service. Data would be uploaded to the data warehouse every week. Every time the data is uploaded, checks would be made to ensure that the data is not corrupted. If the data is corrupted, the uploaded data has to be removed. The upload process and data corruption check process must not impact the processes running against the warehouse. The company decides to configure database-level auditing and set a retention period as part of the implementation process. Would this meet the requirement?
A. Yes
B. No

Correct Answer: B

152. You have a new Azure subscription.
You create an Azure SQL Database instance named DB1 on an Azure SQL Database server named Server1.
You need to ensure that users can connect to DB1 in the event of an Azure regional outage. In the event of an outage, applications that connect to DB1 must be able to connect without having to update the connection strings.
Which two actions should you perform? Each correct answer presents part of the solution.
NOTE: Each correct selection is worth one point.
A. From the properties of DB1, configure geo-replication.
B. From the properties of Server1, add a failover group.
C. Create a new Azure SQL Database server named Server2.
D. From the properties of Server1, configure retention for DB1.
E. Create a new Azure SQL Database instance named DB2.

Correct Answer: B, C

153. A company is planning to use the Azure SQL data warehouse service. Data would be uploaded to the data warehouse every week. Every time the data is uploaded, checks would be made to ensure that the data is not corrupted. If the data is corrupted, the uploaded data has to be removed. The upload process and data corruption check process must not impact the processes running against the warehouse. The company decides to create user-defined restore points before the data is uploaded. And then delete the restore point after the data corruption checks are complete. Would this meet the requirement?
A. Yes
B. No

Correct Answer: A

154. You have two Azure SQL Database servers named Server1 and Server2. Each server contains an Azure SQL database named Database1.
You need to restore Database1 from Server1 to Server2. The solution must replace the existing Database1 on Server2.

Solution: From the Azure portal, you delete Database1 from Server2, and then you create a new database on Server2 by using the backup of Database1 from Server1.
Does this meet the goal?
A. Yes
B. No

Correct Answer: A

155. A company is planning to use the Azure SQL data warehouse service. Data would be uploaded to the data warehouse every week. Every time the data is uploaded, checks would be made to ensure that the data is not corrupted. If the data is corrupted, the uploaded data has to be removed. The upload process and data corruption check process must not impact the processes running against the warehouse. The company decides to configure transactions and then perform a rollback if data corruption is detected. Would this meet the requirement?
A. Yes
B. No

Correct Answer: B

156. You have two Azure SQL Database servers named Server1 and Server2. Each server contains an Azure SQL database named Database1.
You need to restore Database1 from Server1 to Server2. The solution must replace the existing Database1 on Server2.
Solution: You run the Remove-AzSqlDatabase PowerShell cmdlet for Database1 on Server2. You run the Restore-AzSqlDatabase PowerShell cmdlet for
Database1 on Server2.
Does this meet the goal?
A. Yes
B. No

Correct Answer: B

157. A company wants to engineer a solution. The solution would have the following requirements. Ingest data from an on-premise SQL Server. Create pipelines that can integrate data and also run notebooks. Be able to develop notebooks that can be used to transform data. Be able to load the data into a massive parallel processing data for analysis. Which of the following would you use as the service to integrate the on-premise data onto the cloud?
A. Azure Databricks
B. Azure Data Factory
C. Azure SQL Data warehouse
D. Azure Batch

Correct Answer: B

158. You have two Azure SQL Database servers named Server1 and Server2. Each server contains an Azure SQL database named Database1.
You need to restore Database1 from Server1 to Server2. The solution must replace the existing Database1 on Server2.
Solution: You restore Database1 from Server1 to the Server2 by using the RESTORE Transact-SQL command and the REPLACE option.
Does this meet the goal?
A. Yes
B. No

Correct Answer: A

159. A company wants to engineer a solution. The solution would have the following requirements. Ingest data from an on-premise SQL Server. Create pipelines that can integrate data and also run notebooks. Be able to develop notebooks that can be used to transform data. Be able to load the data into a massive parallel processing data for analysis. Which of the following would you use as the service to develop notebooks to transform the data?
A. Azure Databricks
B. Azure Data Factory C
C. Azure SQL Data warehouse
D. Azure Batch

Correct Answer: A

160. A company wants to engineer a solution. The solution would have the following requirements. Ingest data from an on-premise SQL Server. Create pipelines that can integrate data and also run notebooks. Be able to develop notebooks that can be used to transform data. Be able to load the data into a massive parallel processing data for analysis. Which of the following would you use as the service to run notebooks?
A. Azure Databricks
B. Azure Data Factory
C. Azure SQL Data warehouse
D. Azure Batch

Correct Answer: A

161. A company wants to engineer a solution. The solution would have the following requirements. Ingest data from an on-premise SQL Server. Create pipelines that can integrate data and also run notebooks. Be able to develop notebooks that can be used to transform data. Be able to load the data into a massive parallel processing data for analysis. Which of the following would you use as the service to load the data?
A. Azure Databricks
B. Azure Data Factory
C. Azure SQL Data warehouse
D. Azure Batch

Correct Answer: B

162. A company wants to engineer a solution. The solution would have the following requirements. Ingest data from an on-premise SQL Server.
Create pipelines that can integrate data and also run notebooks. Be able to develop notebooks that can be used to transform data. Be able to load the data into a massive parallel processing data for analysis. Which of the following would you use as the service to store the transformed data?
A. Azure Databricks
B. Azure Data Factory
C. Azure SQL Data warehouse
D. Azure Batch

Correct Answer: C

163. Your company currently has a solution in place. This solution consists of streaming data being sent to Azure Event Hubs. The data is then stored in Azure Blob storage. The data contains social media posts. You have to count the number of times the keyword Whizlabs is mentioned in each post every 30 seconds. The data then needs to be available to Microsoft BI in near real-time. You have to implement the new requirement for the solution. You decide to use Azure Databricks to create a Scala notebook. You then create a structured streaming job to connect to the event hub. This would count the number of keywords in the post. The number is then written to a Delta table. You then go ahead to consume the data in PowerBI by using DirectQuery Mode. Would this fulfill the requirement?
A. Yes
B. No

Correct Answer: B

164. You have an Always On availability group deployed to Azure virtual machines. The availability group contains a database named DB1 and has two nodes named SQL1 and SQL2. SQL1 is the primary replica.
You need to initiate a full backup of DB1 on SQL2. Which statement should you run?
A. BACKUP DATABASE DB1 TO URL='https://mystorageaccount.blob.core.windows.net/mycontainer/DB1.bak' with (Differential, STATS=5, COMPRESSION);
B. BACKUP DATABASE DB1 TO URL='https://mystorageaccount.blob.core.windows.net/mycontainer/DB1.bak' with (COPY_ONLY, STATS=5, COMPRESSION);
C. BACKUP DATABASE DB1 TO URL='https://mystorageaccount.blob.core.windows.net/mycontainer/DB1.bak' with (File_Snapshot, STATS=5, COMPRESSION);
D. BACKUP DATABASE DB1 TO URL='https://mystorageaccount.blob.core.windows.net/mycontainer/DB1.bak' with (NoInit, STATS=5, COMPRESSION);

Correct Answer: B

165. Your company currently has a solution in place. This solution consists of streaming data being sent to Azure Event Hubs. The data is then stored in Azure Blob storage. The data contains social media posts. You have to count the number of times the keyword Whizlabs is mentioned in each post every 30 seconds. The data then needs to be available to Microsoft BI in near real-time. You have to implement the new

requirement for the solution. You decide to create an Azure Stream Analytics job. This would use Azure Event Hubs as the input stream. This would count the keywords and send the data to an Azure SQL Database. The data is then consumed in PowerBI by using DirectQuery Mode. Would this fulfill the requirement?
A. Yes
B. No

Correct Answer: A

166. Your company currently has a solution in place. This solution consists of streaming data being sent to Azure Event Hubs. The data is then stored in Azure Blob storage. The data contains social media posts. You have to count the number of times the keyword Whizlabs is mentioned in each post every 30 seconds. The data then needs to be available to Microsoft BI in near real-time. You have to implement the new requirement for the solution. You plan to use Azure Data Factory and an event trigger to detect when new blobs are added to the storage account. You then filter the data in Azure Data Factory and then send the data to an Azure SQL Database. The data is then consumed in PowerBI by using DirectQuery Mode. Would this fulfill the requirement?
A. Yes
B. No

Correct Answer: B

167. You have an Azure subscription that contains an Azure SQL database named SQL1.
SQL1 is in an Azure region that does not support availability zones.
You need to ensure that you have a secondary replica of SQL1 in the same region.
What should you use?
A. log shipping
B. active geo-replication
C. Microsoft SQL Server failover clusters
D. auto-failover groups

Correct Answer: B

168. A company wants to set up a set of data stores on Azure. Each datastore has different requirements. Datastorel – This datastore must be able to store JSON related data. It must also have the ability to replicate data to multiple regions. Datastore2 – This would behave as an OLTP store. Datastore3 – On this data store, one should be able to run queries across petabytes of data. Datastore4 – This store should be able to ingest large amounts of images per day. Which of the following technology would you use for Datastore1?
A. Azure SQL Database
B. Azure Cosmos DB
C. Azure SQL Data Warehouse
D. Azure Data Lake Storage

Correct Answer: B

169. A company wants to set up a set of data stores on Azure. Each datastore has different requirements. Datastore1 – This datastore must be able to store JSON related data. It must also have the ability to replicate data to multiple regions. Datastore2 – This would behave as an OLTP store. Datastore3 – On this data store, one should be able to run queries across petabytes of data. Datastore4 – This store should be able to ingest large amounts of images per day. Which of the following technology would you use for Datastore2?
A. Azure SQL Database
B. Azure Cosmos DB
C. Azure SQL Data Warehouse
D. Azure Data Lake Storage

Correct Answer: A

170. You have an Azure subscription that contains two instances of SQL Server on Azure Virtual Machines named VM1 and VM2. Both instances run Microsoft SQL Server 2019 CU8.
You need to deploy a failover cluster instance (FCI) to VM1 and VM2 that will use Azure shared disks. The solution must maximize resiliency.
Which quorum option should you use?
A. node majority with a cloud witness
B. node majority with no witness
C. node majority with a file share witness
D. node majority with a disk witness

Correct Answer: D

171. A company wants to set up a set of data stores on Azure. Each datastore has different requirements. Datastore1 – This datastore must be able to store JSON related data. It must also have the ability to replicate data to multiple regions. Datastore2 – This would behave as an OLTP store. Datastore3 – On this data store, one should be able to run queries across petabytes of data. Datastore4 – This store should be able to ingest large amounts of images per day. Which of the following technology would you use for Datastore3?
A. Azure SQL Database
B. Azure Cosmos DB
C. Azure SQL Data Warehouse
D. Azure Data Lake Storage

Correct Answer: C

172. You have an Azure SQL database named DB1.
You need to ensure that DB1 will support automatic failover without data loss if a datacenter fails. The solution must minimize costs.
Which deployment option and pricing tier should you configure?
A. Azure SQL Database Premium
B. Azure SQL Database serverless
C. Azure SQL Database Basic
D. Azure SQL Database Hyperscale

Correct Answer: A

173. A company wants to set up a set of data stores on Azure. Each datastore has different requirements. Datastore1 – This datastore must be able to store JSON related data. It must also have the ability to replicate data to multiple regions. Datastore2 – This would behave as an OLTP store. Datastore3 – On this data store, one should be able to run queries across petabytes of data. Datastore4 – This store should be able to ingest large amounts of images per day. Which of the following technology would you use for Datastore4?
A. Azure SQL Database
B. Azure Cosmos DB
C. Azure SQL Data Warehouse
D. Azure Data Lake Storage

Correct Answer: D

174. You have an Azure SQL database named DB1.
You need to ensure that DB1 will support automatic failover without data loss if a datacenter fails. The solution must minimize costs.
Which deployment option and pricing tier should you configure?
A. Azure SQL Database Business Critical
B. Azure SQL Database Standard
C. Azure SQL Database managed instance General Purpose
D. Azure SQL Database Hyperscale

Correct Answer: A

175. A company plans to use the Azure Databricks service. They want to create persistent clusters that would support auto-scaling for analytical processes.
The company decides to create a Standard cluster. Would this fulfill the requirement?
A. Yes
B. No

Correct Answer: B

176. You plan to deploy two instances of SQL Server on Azure virtual machines in a highly available configuration that will use an Always On availability group.
You need to recommend a deployment solution that meets the following requirements:
•Provides a Service Level Agreement (SLA) of at least 99.95%
•Replicates databases in the same group synchronously
•Minimizes the latency of database writes
What should you recommend?
A. Create two proximity groups and two availability sets. Deploy each virtual machine to a unique availability set. Add one virtual machine to each proximity group.
B. Create a proximity group and an availability set. Deploy each virtual machine to the availability set. Add both virtual machines to the proximity group.

C. Create a proximity group and two availability sets. Deploy each virtual machine to a unique availability set. Add both virtual machines to the proximity group.
D. Create two proximity groups and a single availability set. Deploy both virtual machines to the availability set. Add one virtual machine to each proximity group.

Correct Answer: B

177. A company plans to use the Azure Databricks service. They want to create persistent clusters that would support auto-scaling for analytical processes. The company decides to create a High concurrency cluster. Would this fulfill the requirement?
A. Yes
B. No

Correct Answer: A

178. A company plans to use the Azure Databricks service. They want to create persistent clusters that would support auto-scaling for analytical processes. The company decides to create a Premium cluster. Would this fulfill the requirement?
A. Yes
B. No

Correct Answer: B

179. A company is designing a complete end-to-end solution for data analytics. The overall architecture is given below.

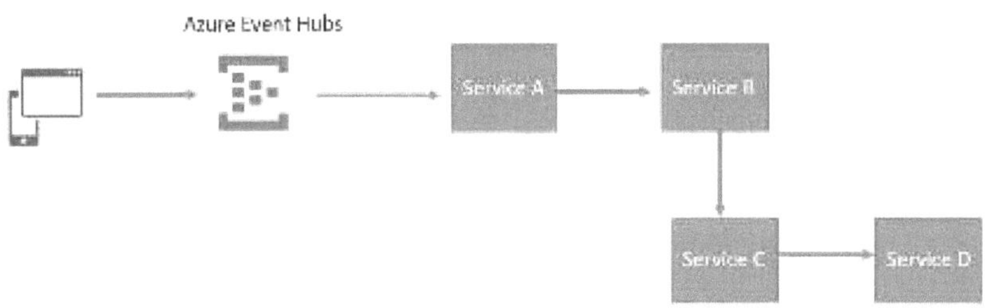

Azure Event Hubs would be used to ingest data from multiple devices. The data needs to be processed by Service A and sent to a relational store service by Service B. Every month, an ETL service (Service C) needs to run and store the output data in a columnar data store hosted by Service D. Which of the following would you use as Service A?
A. Azure SQL Database
B. Azure Stream Analytics
C. Azure SQL Data Warehouse
D. Azure Data Factory

Correct Answer: B

180. You have a single availability set that contains two SQL Server on Azure Virtual Machines instances.

The instances were deployed by using an Azure Marketplace SQL Server 2019 Enterprise image that has the latest cumulative updates applied. The instances are configured as the nodes of a failover cluster instance (FCI) named FCI1.
You need to ensure that client applications can connect to FCI1. The solution must meet the following requirements:
•Provide an availability SLA.
•Minimize costs.
What should you create?
A. an Azure Standard Load Balancer
B. a virtual network name (VNN) resource
C. a Basic Azure Load Balancer
D. a distributed network name (DNN) resource

Correct Answer: D

181. You have an Azure subscription that contains two Azure SQL managed instances named SQLMI1 and SQLMI2. SQLMI1 contains a database named DB1 and a user named User1.
User1 drops DB1.
You need to perform a point-in-time restore of DB1 to SQLMI2.
What should you use to perform the restore?
A. Azure CLI
B. Transact-SQL
C. the Azure portal
D. Azure PowerShell

Correct Answer: C

182. You deploy an instance of SQL Server on Azure Virtual Machines: named SQL1 that hosts multiple databases.
You configure the full recovery model for all the databases.
You perform a full backup of the master database on SQL1.
You need to a perform an additional backup of the master database on SQL1. The solution must minimize how long it takes to perform the backup.
Which type of backup should you perform?
A. log
B. full
C. differential
D. tail-log

Correct Answer: C

183. HOTSPOT You are planning the migration of the SERVER1 databases. The solution must meet the business requirements. What should you include in the migration plan? To answer, select the appropriate options in the answer area. NOTE: Each correct selection is worth one point.

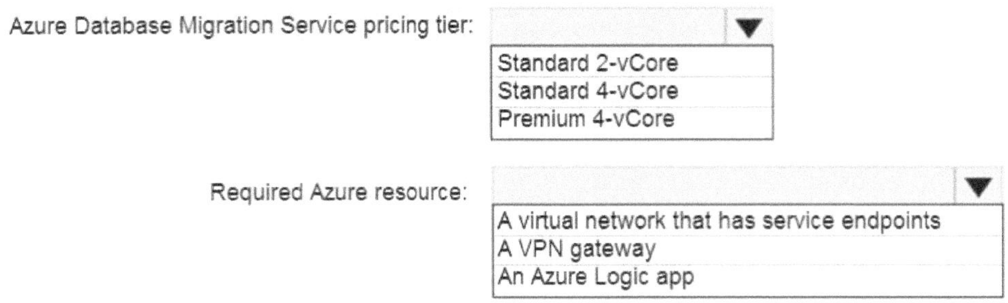

Correct Answer:

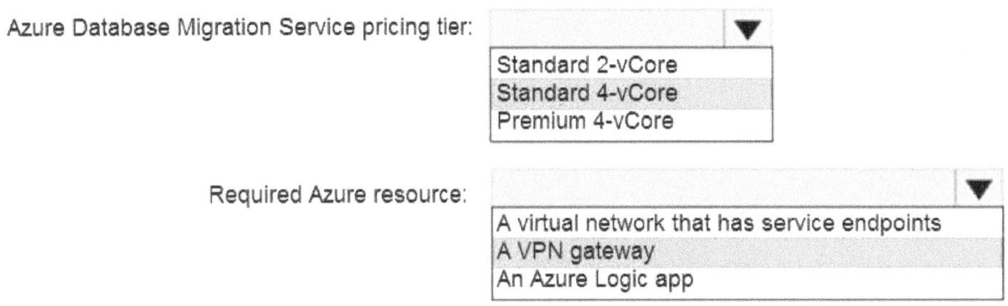

184. A company is designing a complete end-to-end solution for data analytics. The overall architecture is given below.

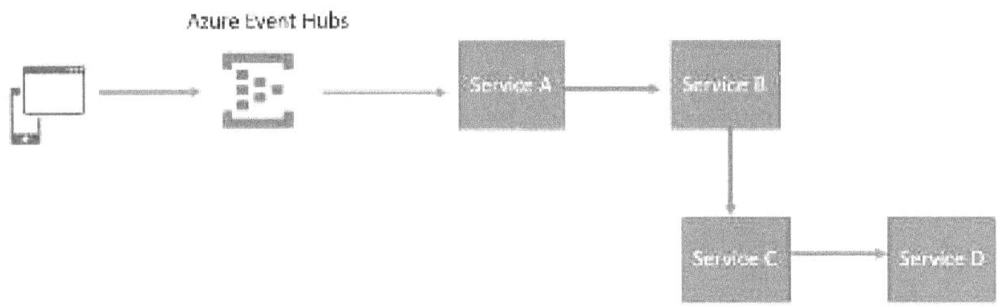

Azure Event Hubs would be used to ingest data from multiple devices. The data needs to be processed by Service A and sent to a relational store services by Service B. Every month, an ETL service (Service C) needs to run and store the output data in a columnar data store hosted by Service D. Which of the following would you use as Service B?

A. Azure SQL Database
B. Azure Stream Analytics
C. Azure SQL Data Warehouse
D. Azure Data Factory

Correct Answer: A

185. DRAG DROP You need to configure user authentication for the SERVER1 databases. The solution must meet the security and compliance requirements. Which three actions should you perform in sequence? To answer, move the appropriate actions from the list of actions to the answer area and arrange them in the correct order.

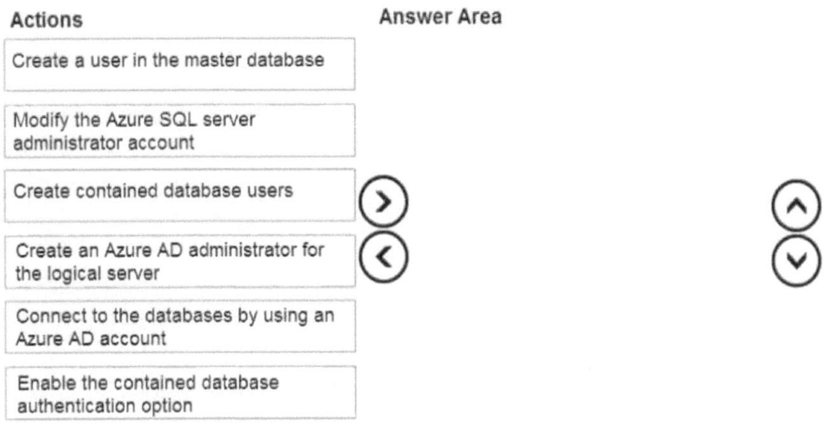

Correct Answer:

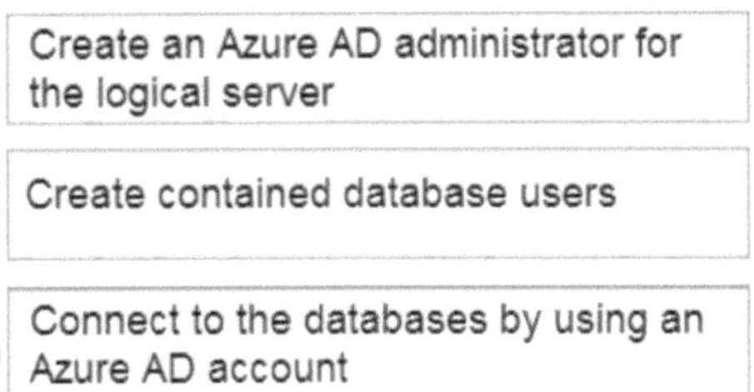

186. You need to identify the cause of the performance issues on SalesSQLDb1. Which two dynamic management views should you use? Each correct answer presents part of the solution. NOTE: Each correct selection is worth one point.
A. sys.dm_pdw_nodes_tran_locks
B. sys.dm_exec_compute_node_errors
C. sys.dm_exec_requests
D. sys.dm_cdc_errors
E. sys.dm_pdw_nodes_os_wait_stats
F. sys.dm_tran_locks

Correct Answer: A, E

187. A company is designing a complete end-to-end solution for data analytics. The overall architecture is given below.

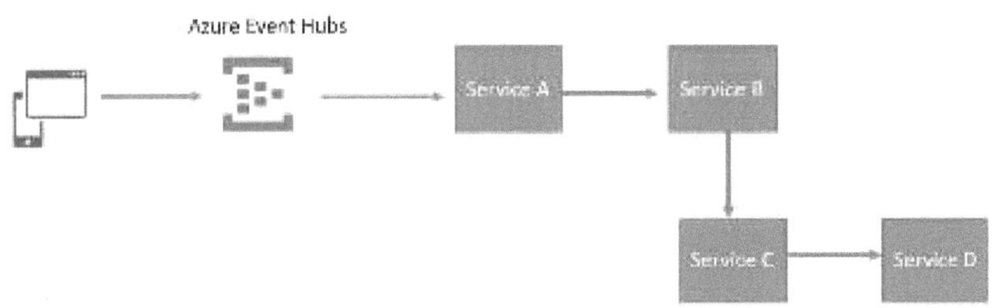

Azure Event Hubs would be used to ingest data from multiple devices. The data needs to be processed by Service A and sent to a relational store services by Service B. Every month, an ETL service (Service C)

needs to run and store the output data in a columnar data store hosted by Service D. Which of the following would you use as Service C?
A. Azure SQL Database
B. Azure Stream Analytics
C. Azure SQL Data Warehouse
D. Azure Data Factory Explanation:

Correct Answer: D

188. A company is designing a complete end-to-end solution for data analytics. The overall architecture is given below.

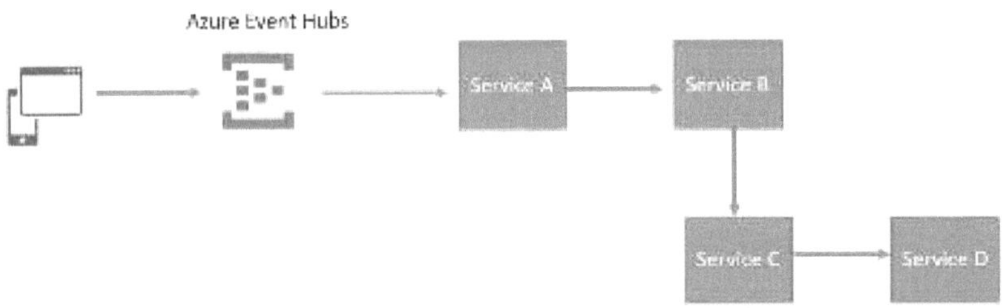

Azure Event Hubs would be used to ingest data from multiple devices. The data needs to be processed by Service A and sent to a relational store services by Service B. Every month, an ETL service (Service C) needs to run and store the output data in a columnar data store hosted by Service D. Which of the following would you use as Service D?
A. Azure SQL Database
B. Azure Stream Analytics
C. Azure SQL Data Warehouse
D. Azure Data Factory

Correct Answer: C

189. You are designing a multi-tenant enterprise data warehouse using Azure Synapse that holds some crucial data for a Medical and health Insurance company. This data relates to sensitive Protected Health information about patients' ailments and diagnoses.
You need to create a solution to provide Health information management professionals the ability to view all basic entries in patients such as Name, Home Address, and Email.
The solution must avert all Health information management professionals from viewing or inferring demographic information, medical histories, test and laboratory results, mental health conditions, and insurance information.
What should you include to complete this requirement?
A. Data Masking
B. Always Encrypted
C. Transparent Data Encryption
D. Row-level security

Correct Answer: D

190. A company is planning to set an Azure SQL database. The database contains a table that will be storing sensitive Personally Identifiable Information (PII) data. The company wants to have the ability to track and store all the queries that are executed against the PII data. The company database administrator decides to add classifications to the columns that contain sensitive data. Auditing is also turned on for the database. Would this fulfill the requirement?
A. Yes
B. No

Correct Answer: A

191. You have a dedicated virtual machine that monitors and collects data from SQL Server instance on Azure to investigate performance issues.
The dedicated machine has the following components installed.
• Azure Monitor Agent
• Workload Insights extension
To get started with SQL Insights, from the Monitor blade, we create a profile after selecting SQL (preview).
Name the component we need to configure from "Create profile Page" that would help to send all monitoring data.
A. Monitoring profile
B. Collection settings
C. Log Analytics workspace
D. Azure Activity Log

Correct Answer: C

192. A company is planning to set an Azure SQL database. The database contains a table that will be storing sensitive Personally Identifiable Information (PII) data. The company wants to have the ability to track and store all the queries that are executed against the PII data. The company database administrator decides to create a SELECT trigger on the table in the database. This trigger will write data to a new table in the database. A stored procedure would then be executed to lookup column classifications and perform joins. Would this fulfill the requirement?
A. Yes
B. No

Correct Answer: B

193. You have an Azure subscription and along with it you have a SQL Server Database which is causing a lot of performance issues.
You have set up an extended events engine in Azure SQL which is a lightweight and powerful monitoring system that allows you to capture granular information about activity in your databases and servers.
Which Channel within the Extended event is typically related to performance?
A. Admin Events
B. Operational Events
C. Analytic Events
D. Debug Events

Correct Answer: C

194. You have a Microsoft Azure Subscription that holds an Azure SQL Managed Instance. This holds tables on various modules of an ERP system. You need to configure automatic tuning on the Azure SQL Managed Instance. Which Automatic tuning option is available for Instance database support?
A. FORCE_LAST_GOOD_PLAN
B. CREATE INDEX
C. DROP INDEX
D. CREATE PRIMARY KEY CONSTRAINT

Correct Answer: A

195. You have an Azure SQL server virtual machine.
You need to back up the transaction log from the Primary server instance to the secondary server instance. Which option should you choose?
A. Implement 'Always On' availability groups
B. Configure transactional replication
C. Configure Transaction Log Shipping
D. Import a DACPAC

Correct Answer: C

196. A company is planning to set an Azure SQL database. The database contains a table that will be storing sensitive Personally Identifiable Information (PII) data. The company wants to have the ability to track and store all the queries that are executed against the PII data. The company decides to implement Transparent Data Encryption. Would this fulfill the requirement?
A. Yes
B. No

Correct Answer: B

197. A company wants a Cosmos DB accounts. Below are the requirements for the account. Be able to store millions of objects. The data stored will contain information about users. The company should have the ability to identity and query relationships between users. Which of the following could be used as the API for the Cosmos DB account?
A. MongoDB
B. Table
C. Gremlin
D. Cassandra

Correct Answer: C

198. A company is making use of an Azure SQL database. The database administrator is documenting the procedure for the automated backups which are taken by the SQL database service. Which of the following is the first type of backup that is taken by the service?

A. A full weekly backup
B. A full daily backup
C. A differential weekly backup
D. A differential daily backup

Correct Answer: A

199. You have a 'server01' running HADR with a primary role and it crashes. The DBA performs a HADR takeover by force on the 'servers02' to switch roles. The 'server02' now becomes the primary server. The below DMVs provide information on the state of a replica. Match the correct definition with their respective DMVs.

	DMV'S		ANSWER AREA
1	sys.dm_hadr_availability_replica_states	A	Returns a row for each Always On availability replica of all Always On availability groups
2	sys.dm_hadr_database_replica_states	B	Returns a row for each local replica and a row for each remote replica in the same Always On availability group
3	sys.dm_hadr_database_replica_cluster_states	C	Returns a row for each database that is participating in an Always On availability group for which the local instance of SQL Server is hosting an availability replica
4	sys.dm_hadr_availability_replica_cluster_states	D	Returns a row containing information intended to provide you with insight into the health of the available databases in the Always On availability groups in each Always On availability group on the Windows Server Failover Clustering cluster

Correct Answer: 1-B, 2-C, 3-D and 4-A

200. A company is making use of an Azure SQL database. The database administrator documents the procedure for the automated backups taken by the SQL database service. Which of the following is the third type of backup that is taken by the service?
A. A full daily backup
B. A differential backup taken from the last 12 hours
C. Differential backups taken since the last full backup
D. Log backups taken since the last full backup

Correct Answer: B

201. A company is making use of an Azure SQL database. The database administrator is documenting the procedure for the automated backups which are taken by the SQL database service. Which of the following is the first type of backup that is taken by the service?
A. Log backups taken since the last full backup
B. Log backups taken since the last differential backup
C. A differential backup taken from the last 12 hours
D. Differential backups taken since the last full backup

Correct Answer: B

199. You have a Microsoft Azure SQL database instance. The data size is large. You are facing issues with storage, computing resources, and network while maintaining the performance of the database.
To solve this issue, you have implemented Database sharding where you divide a data store into a set of horizontal partitions or shards. Each shard has the same schema but holds a distinct subset of the data. Match the below sharding strategies that are commonly used when selecting the shard key and decide how to distribute data across shards.

PERFORMANCE TECHNIQUES		ANSWER AREA
Lookup strategy	A	In this strategy groups related items together in the same shard and orders them by shard key—the shard keys are sequential. It's useful for applications that frequently retrieve sets of items using these queries
Range strategy	B	The purpose of this strategy is to reduce the chance of hotspots (shards that receive a disproportionate amount of load). It distributes the data across the shards in a way that achieves a balance between the size of each shard and the average load that each shard will encounter. The sharding logic computes the shard to store an item based on a hash of one or more attributes of the data.
Hash strategy	C	In this strategy, the sharding logic implements a map that routes a request for data to the shard that contains that data using the shard key. In a multi-tenant application, all the data for a tenant might be stored together in a shard using the tenant ID as the shard key

Correct Answer: 1-C, 2-A and 3-B

200. You have to design a solution for your company. The solution would involve the following components. Processing of streams of data from multiple IoT based devices. Processing of streaming data. Storage of output data in a JSON based data store. You have to decide on the ideal store for storing the JSON based documents.
You decide to implement a Cosmos DB Account using the SQL API Would this fulfill the requirement?
A. Yes
B. No

Correct Answer: A

201. You have a large production Azure SQL database named 'bankdb'. You are running a reporting or analytics workload on this data that is causing performance issues.

To overcome this issue you decide to have a second database such that additional workload can be handled thereby minimizing the performance impact on your production workload. Data Sync helps you to keep the two databases synchronized. Below are the steps required to set up SQL Data Sync between databases. Identify the correct sequence from the options below.
A. Add a Database in Azure SQL Database
B. Add a SQL Server Database
C. Create a Sync group
D. Configure Sync Group
E. Add Sync Member

Correct Answer: C, E, A, B and D

202. You have to design a solution for your company. The solution would involve the following components. Processing of streams of data from multiple IoT based devices. Processing of streaming data. Storage of output data in a JSON based data store.
You have to decide on the ideal store for storing the JSON based documents. You decide to implement Azure Event Hubs for the storage of JSON documents. Would this fulfill the requirement?
A. Yes
B. No

Correct Answer: B

203. A company is planning to deploy thousands of IoT enabled devices. The data from these devices will be sent to an Azure Event Hub instance. The data from this instance must then be transferred to Power BI for real-time visualizations. Which of the following service can be used to complete this system?
A. Azure HDInsight with Spark Streaming
B. Apache Spark
C. Azure Stream Analytics
D. Azure Functions

Correct Answer: C

204. You have an Azure SQL manage instance that has a database named IBC-data that stores data in geo-redundant storage blobs which are replicated to a paired region. Match the following storage redundancies for backup.

BACKUP STORAGE REDUNDANCIES		ANSWER AREA
Locally redundant storage (LRS)	A	Copying your backups synchronously three times within a single physical location in the primary region using LRS. Then it copies your data asynchronously three times to a single physical location in the paired secondary region.
Zone-redundant storage (ZRS)	B	Copies your backups synchronously across three Azure availability zones in the primary region.
Geo-redundant storage (GRS)	C	Copies your backups synchronously three times within a single physical location in the primary region

Correct Answer: 1-C, 2-B and 3-A

205. A company has purchased a number of IoT devices. An IoT appliance is used to communicate with the IoT devices. The company needs a solution to monitor the devices in real-time. Which of the following can be used for this requirement?
A. Azure Data Factory
B. Azure Stream Analytics Edge
C. Azure Analysis Services
D. Azure Event Hubs

Correct Answer: B

206. Your company is making use of an Azure SQL database. The database comes under heavy load during the last month of the year. You need to scale the Azure SQL database during this time manually. Which of the following would you implement for this requirement?
A. Make use of elastic pools.
B. Make use of sharding.
C. Increase the database throughput units.
D. Decrease the database throughput units.

Correct Answer: C

207. You have a Microsoft Azure SQL database instance running in the single-user mode for a POS application that manages sales and performs day to day operations of the retail store. We have a table named product_specification. The non-cluster index is created on columns batch_number, name, description, and price. There was a loss of data due to a deadlock caused when multiple users started performing CRUD operations.
Which parameter option under the DBCC(Database Console Commands) check would ensure an integrity check for the given table with no data loss?
A. NOINDEX
B. REPAIR_FAST
C. REPAIR_REBUILD
D. REPAIR_ALLOW_DATA_LOSS

Correct Answer: C

208. An instance of Microsoft Azure SQL Server has a Sales Database with multiple objects. You have multiple indexes created on tables. Index pages are increasing massively because of the Insert and Update operation.
Name a stored procedure that provides all information about the fragmentation page and space.
A. dm_db_index_physical_stats
B. dm_db_column_store_row_group_physical_stats
C. dm_db_index_usage_stats
D. dm_db_index_operational_stats

Correct Answer: A

209. A company wants to use an Azure SQL Data warehouse instance. They need to load millions of rows of data into the warehouse every day. Staging tables have been set up for the data load process. Which of the following should be used as the staging table type to optimize the data loading process?
A. Round-robin
B. Hash-distributed
C. Replicated
D. External

Correct Answer: A

210. Your company wants to create a real-time monitoring application. It would alert users when an IoT enabled device travels more than 50 meters away from a particular location.
You have to design an Azure Stream Analytics job to process the data and implement the requirement. You have to minimize the amount of code developed and the number of technologies used for this requirement. Which of the following would you use as the Input type?
A. Stream
B. Reference
C. Event Hub
D. Azure Functions

Correct Answer: A

211. You need to run a Transact-SQL system stored procedure on the Microsoft Azure job agent database. For this, we need to add a new target server member to the target group containing server(s) and exclude a database target member MappingDB from the server target group. Identify the procedure that would help us perform the above tasks.
A. jobs.target_groups
B. jobs.sp_add_target_group
C. jobs.sp_add_target_group_member
D. jobs.target_group_members

Correct Answer: C

212. Your company wants to create a real-time monitoring application. It would alert users when an IoT enabled device travels more than 50 meters away from a particular location. You have to design an Azure Stream Analytics job to process the data and implement the requirement. You have to minimize the amount of code developed and the number of technologies used for this requirement. Which of the following would you use as the Input Source?
A. Azure IoT Hub
B. Azure Event Hubs
C. Azure Blob Storage
D. Azure Functions

Correct Answer: A

213. We have a SQL Server on an Azure VM named CHC-DB-SERVER which holds databases such as RV Medicare, and Medicaid for various clients of an insurance claim company. You add a user as a member of the sysadmin group who would be the SQL Agent operator such that it receives emails as an alert on every job failure. You need to perform certain actions from the below options to achieve the requirement.

A. Create a Job Alert
B. Enable Database Mail
C. Create a Job Notification
D. Enable Email setting for SQL Server Agent
E. Create a targeted Job

Correct Answers: B, D and E

212. Your company wants to create a real-time monitoring application. It would alert users when an IoT enabled device travels more than 50 meters away from a particular location. You have to design an Azure Stream Analytics job to process the data and implement the requirement. You have to minimize the amount of code developed and the number of technologies used for this requirement.

Which of the following would you use as the underlying Function in Azure Stream Analytics?

A. A.Aggregate
B. B.Sum
C. C.Windowing
D. D.Geospatial

Correct Answer: D

213. You have a Microsoft Azure SQL server virtual machine. You wish to install log shipping such that you could store backups on a dedicated SMTP file share. You need to configure servers to perform the Log Shipping step. Which server instance would you choose to configure and perform actions such as complete backup job & copy backup Job You can choose the same server instance for different actions performed?

A. Monitor Server Instance
B. Primary Server Instance
C. Secondary Server Instance
D. Backup Share file Server

Correct Answers: B, C

214. A company wants to design a processing system. The system has the following requirements. Data would be sent from IoT enabled devices. The solution must be able to ingest high volumes of data. The data needs to be analyzed in real-time. Query-based solutions must be deployed using continuous integration. Data must be visualized using graphs. Which of the following would you implement for this requirement? Choose 2 Correct Answers from the options given below.

A. Use Azure Analysis Services to query the data and send the query results to Power BI.
B. Use an Azure Event Hub to capture the data and send the data to Azure Data Lake Storage
C. Make sure the IoT devices send data to Azure Event Hub

D. Use Azure Stream Analytics to query the data and output to Power BI. Use Azure Pipelines to deploy the Azure Stream Analytics Solution

Correct Answer: C, D

215. I want to compress my table dbo.myTable. I start with the following code:
• ALTER TABLE dbo.myTable
• REBUILD PARTITION = ALL
• WITH (DATA_COMPRESSION =
Which of the options is NOT a valid ending to this code?
A. PAGE)
B. ROW)
C. NONE)
D. PREFIX)

Correct Answer: D

216. A company has an Azure storage account that has over a million files. These files are going to be shared with an external partner organization. The organization will analyze the files over the duration of 3 months. You have to recommend an access solution for the files which fit the following requirements. Ensure that ONLY the partner organization can access the files. Ensure that the access is revoked ONLY for partner organization after 3 months.
Which of the following would you implement for this requirement?
A. Shared Access Keys
B. Management Policies
C. Account Keys
D. Shared Access Signatures

Correct Answer: D

217. You plan to create a table in an Azure Synapse Analytics dedicated SQL pool. The data in the table is invoice data under the sales schema for the past 3 years. SQL Monitor has raised a "Long running query" which when executed showed details about all invoices generated over years to gather month-wise sales for individual items. Due to this management decided to purge data, once a year for data that is older than three years.
Using which of the options below can you ensure that data can be distributed evenly across partitions such that the operation of purging data is accelerated?
A. Filegroup
B. Partition scheme
C. Partition Function
D. Partition Column

Correct Answer: C

218. company is planning to use an Azure SQL data warehouse. They have 2 fact tables named whizlab_sales and whizlab_invoice. Below are the details on each table. whizlab_sales The table would

be 500 GB in size. A column named SalesDate would be used extensively in the WHERE clause in queries. A column named SalesProduct would be used extensively in JOIN operations. A column named SalesRegion is used for grouping. Around 75% of the records are related to one of the 40 region values of the SalesRegion column. whizlab_invoice The table would be 6 GB in size. A column named SalesDate and SalesProduct would be used extensively in the WHERE clause in queries. A column named SalesRegion is used for grouping. You need to ensure that query performance is optimized for each table. Which of the following would you use as the Distribution type for the whizlab_sales table?
A. External
B. Hash-distributed
C. Round-robin
D. Primary

Correct Answer: B

219. You plan to create a table and you need to establish trust around the integrity of data stored. Ledger provides a chronicle of all alternates made to the database over time. Choose the right option that best defines the ledger table.
A. Implements Row level security
B. Implements Encryption of data.
C. Implements decryption of data
D. Preserves historical data in the history table.

Correct Answer: D

220. You have SQL Server on an Azure virtual machine that contains a database named DB1. Consider a table that holds coffee inventory data.
The columns within the table are ID, Name, Price description and Create Date.
We have a non-clustered index on our Name column and the query is Sargable. We also add non-key columns such as Price and Description.
The data in the table is not evenly distributed. We have more rows with 'Name' including "Costa Rica".
Following is the stored procedure which basically filters the different coffee entries from the table.
DROP PROCEDURE IF EXISTS dbo.FilterCoffee
GO;
CREATE PROCEDURE dbo.FilterCoffee
@ParamCountry varchar(30)
AS
BEGIN
SELECT Name, Price, Description From dbo.FilterCoffee Where Name lile @ParamCountry + '%'
END
GO
Executing the procedure twice with different parameter values 'Costa Rica' and then 'Eithopia' receives the same query plan which uses the table scan.
What option would you select that provides a solution to poor performance from parameter sniffing?
A. WITH RECOMPILE option
B. IF/ELSE STATEMENT
C. Run DBCC FREEPROCACHE

D. OPTIMIZE FOR

Correct Answers: A, B and D

221. A company is planning to use an Azure SQL data warehouse. They have 2 fact tables named whizlab_sales and whizlab_invoice. Below are the details on each table. whizlab_sales The table would be 500 GB in size. A column named SalesDate would be used extensively in the WHERE clause in queries. A column named SalesProduct would be used extensively in JOIN operations. A column named SalesRegion is used for grouping. Around 75% of the records are related to one of the 40 region values of the SalesRegion column. whizlab_invoice The table would be 6 GB in size A column named SalesDate and SalesProduct would be used extensively in the WHERE clause in queries. A column named SalesRegion is used for grouping. You need to ensure that query performance is optimized for each table. Which of the following would you use as the Distribution column for the whizlab_sales table?
A. SalesDate
B. SalesProduct
C. SalesRegion
D. SalesID

Correct Answer: B

222. London Heathrow Airport is one of the busiest in Europe by passenger traffic. To keep adverse weather, aircraft delays, traffic-clogged highways, public transport slow-downs, and global pandemics from disrupting its operational readiness, and to identify the untapped capacity that it can use to grow sustainably, Heathrow needs an effectively managed data estate. Which Microsoft Azure service would help derive data-driven insights to optimize its operations, support continued growth, and improve air travel experiences?
A. Data Catalog
B. Microsoft Purview
C. Azure Lighthouse
D. Azure CycleCloud

Correct Answer: B

223. A company is planning to use an Azure SQL data warehouse. They have 2 fact tables named whizlab_sales and whizlab_invoice. Below are the details on each table. whizlab_sales The table would be 500 GB in size. A column named SalesDate would be used extensively in the WHERE clause in queries. A column named SalesProduct would be used extensively in JOIN operations. A column named SalesRegion is used for grouping. Around 75% of the records are related to one of the 40 region values of the SalesRegion column. whizlab_invoice The table would be 6 GB in size A column named SalesDate and SalesProduct would be used extensively in the WHERE clause in queries. A column named SalesRegion is used for grouping. You need to ensure that query performance is optimized for each table. Which of the following would you use as the Distribution type for the whizlab_invoice table?
A. External
B. Hash-distributed
C. Round-robin
D. Primary

Correct Answer: C

224. We have an Azure SQL Database server named IBC_010122 that stores PHI data for customers at Change health care. This data is accessed and transmitted across networks between the database Server and various HealthTech, and InsurTech Client applications. To encrypt data that is transmitted across networks which form of data encryption is most suitable?
A. Always Encrypted
B. TLS
C. TDE
D. CLE

Correct Answer: B

225. A company is planning to use an Azure SQL data warehouse. They have 2 fact tables named whizlab_sales and whizlab_invoice. Below are the details on each table. whizlab_sales The table would be 500 GB in size. A column named SalesDate would be used extensively in the WHERE clause in queries. A column named SalesProduct would be used extensively in JOIN operations. A column named SalesRegion is used for grouping. Around 75% of the records are related to one of the 40 region values of the SalesRegion column. whizlab_invoice The table would be 6 GB in size. A column named SalesDate and SalesProduct would be used extensively in the WHERE clause in queries. A column named SalesRegion is used for grouping. You need to ensure that query performance is optimized for each table. Which of the following would you use as the Distribution column for the whizlab_invoice table?
A. SalesDate
B. SalesProduct
C. SalesRegion
D. SalesID

Correct Answer: C

226. You need to migrate a disk-based table for sales data on a SQL 2014 server to SQL 2016 such that we could have these tables as memory-optimized. A back and restore option was used for this operation. The need for this migration was to improve performance. Determine the Transact-SQL segments you should use such that the performance benefits are concluded and table statistics are updated consequently.

	SQL SEGMENTS
A	Create procedure sp_inventory WITH NATIVE COMPILATION
B	ALTER DATABASE CURRENT SET COMPATIBILITY_LEVEL = 130
C	EXEC sp_inventory
D	UPDATE STATISTICS dbo.sales
E	EXEC sp_recompile N' sp_inventory

Correct Answers: B, D and E

227. A company wants to have a data store in Azure. They want to store data in the form of nodes and relationships between the nodes via graph structures. Which of the following could they use as the data store?
A. Blob storage
B. Cosmos DB
C. Azure Databricks
D. Azure Data Lake storage

Correct Answer: B

228. A company holds a Microsoft cloud subscription. We need to understand how we enable the staff of the company to connect to the cloud services.
We have the Azure virtual network gateway to access the cloud environment.
To ensure a secure connection for all of the users who work at the office, between the data center or office and the Azure virtual network, which of the following VPN option would you choose from below?
A. site to site (S2S) VPN
B. IPSec
C. ExpressRoute
D. point-to-site VPN

Correct Answer: A

229. Your company has an enterprise Data warehouse in Azure Synapse. You have to load data into the SQL data warehouse. You have to ensure that load times are decreased when data is loaded into the tables in the data warehouse. Which of the following would you consider carrying out for this requirement? Choose 2 Correct Answers from the options given below.
A. Running multiple load jobs in parallel
B. Running a single load job at a time.
C. For larger jobs, scaling up the SQL pool before the load operation
D. For larger jobs, scaling down the SQL pool before the load operation

Correct Answer: B, C

230. You have Customer PHI data residing at TIBCO which is a legacy service used to integrate applications using a visual, model-driven development environment by CHC. We need to migrate this data to Azure SQL Database such that we can perform certain analyses.
The TIBCO system produces time series analysis-based reports for customers who are segregated on the basis of aliment diagnosed. There are six ailments on which these analyses would broadly be carried out.
Data from the TIBCO system is stored in Azure Event Hub.
For being affirmative on the diagnosis done for the aliment the reports would be sent to four other departments such that pre-operative assessment and examination tests could be carried out.
Each department has an Azure Web App that displays time series-based assessment and contains a WebJob that processes incoming data from Event Hub.
All Web Apps run on App Service Plans with three instances.
Data throughput must be maximized. Latency must be minimized.

You need to implement the Azure Event Hub. The partition Key is ‘department’. What would be the number of partitions required for optimal data distribution?
A. 3
B. 4
C. 6
D. 12

Correct Answer: C

231. You have a single availability set that contains two SQL Server on Azure Virtual Machines instances. The instances were deployed by using an Azure Marketplace SQL Server 2019 Enterprise image that has the latest cumulative updates applied. The instances are configured as the nodes of a failover cluster instance (FCI) named FCI1.
You need to ensure that client applications can connect to FCI1. The solution must meet the following requirements:
* Provide an availability SLA
* Minimize costs.
What should you create?
A. virtual network name (VNN) resource
B. Basic Azure Load Balancer
C. distributed network name (DNN) resource
D. Azure Standard Load Balancer
Correct Answer: C

232. You have to develop a solution that would make use of Azure Stream Analytics. The Stream Analytics job would be used to load data into an Azure Cosmos DB Account. Which of the following would you use as the underlying API for the Azure Cosmos DB account? A.Gremlin B.Table C.SQL D.Cassandra Explanation: Answer – C
The instances were deployed by using an Azure Marketplace SQL Server 2019 Enterprise image that has the latest cumulative updates applied. The instances are configured as the nodes of a failover cluster instance (FCI) named FCI1.
You need to ensure that client applications can connect to FCI1. The solution must meet the following requirements:
* Provide an availability SLA
* Minimize costs.
What should you create?
A. Aa virtual network name (VNN) resource
B. Ba Basic Azure Load Balancer
C. Ca distributed network name (DNN) resource
D. Dan Azure Standard Load Balancer

Correct Answer: C

233. Your company is planning to use the Azure SQL Database along with elastic pools. The tables in the databases will store customer information. Each record in the table will have a value for the column

CustomerID. You have to partition the data based on the values in the column CustomerID. You decide to separate the data into shards and use horizontal partitioning. Would this fulfill the requirement?
A. Yes
B. No

Correct Answer: A

234. You deploy an instance of SQL Server on Azure Virtual Machines named SQL1 that hosts multiple databases.
You configure the full recovery model for all the databases.
You perform a full backup of the master database on SQL1.
You need to a perform an additional backup of the master database on SQL1. The solution must minimize how long it takes to perform the backup.
Which type of backup should you perform?
A. tail-log
B. differential
C. full
D. log

Correct Answer: B

235. Your company is planning to use the Azure SQL Database along with elastic pools. The tables in the databases will store customer information. Each record in the table will have a value for the column CustomerID. You have to partition the data based on the values in the column CustomerID. You decide to separate the data into regions by using horizontal partitioning. Would this fulfill the requirement?
A. Yes
B. No

Correct Answer: B

236. Your company is planning to use the Azure SQL Database along with elastic pools. The tables in the databases will store customer information. Each record in the table will have a value for the column CustomerID. You have to partition the data based on the values in the column CustomerID.
You decide to separate the data into regions by using vertical partitioning. Would this fulfill the requirement?
A. Yes
B. No

Correct Answer: B

237. You have a single availability set that contains two SQL Server on Azure Virtual Machines instances. The instances were deployed by using an Azure Marketplace SQL Server 2019 Enterprise image that has the latest cumulative updates applied. The instances are configured as the nodes of a failover cluster instance (FCI) named FCI1.
You need to ensure that client applications can connect to FCI1. The solution must meet the following requirements:

* Provide an availability SLA
* Minimize costs.

What should you create?

A. Aa virtual network name (VNN) resource
B. Ba Basic Azure Load Balancer
C. Ca distributed network name (DNN) resource
D. Dan Azure Standard Load Balancer

Correct Answer: C

238. Your company needs to set a Cosmos DB database. An application would be connecting and using the database. The application always needs to see the latest committed write. You need to decide on the ideal consistency level for the database. You decide to set the consistency level to Eventual. Would this fulfill the requirement?

A. Yes
B. No

Correct Answer: B

239. You plan to deploy two instances of SQL Server on Azure virtual machines in a highly available configuration that will use an Always On availability group.

You need to recommend a deployment solution that meets the following requirements:

* Provides a Service Level Agreement (SLA) of at least 99.95%
* Replicates databases in the same group synchronously
* Minimizes the latency of database writes

What should you recommend?

A. Create a proximity group and an availability set. Deploy each virtual machine to the availability set Add both virtual machines to the proximity
B. group.
C. Create two proximity groups and a single availability set. Deploy both virtual machines to the availability set. Add one virtual machine to each proximity group.
D. Create two proximity groups and two availability sets. Deploy each virtual machine to a unique availability set. Add one virtual machine to each proximity group.
E. Create a proximity group and two availability sets. Deploy each virtual machine to a unique availability set. Add both virtual machines to the proximity group.

Correct Answer: A

240. Your company needs to set a Cosmos DB database. An application would be connecting and using the database. The application always needs to see the latest committed write. You need to decide on the ideal consistency level for the database. You decide to set the consistency level to Strong. Would this fulfill the requirement?

A. Yes
B. No

Correct Answer: A

241. You are designing a security model for an Azure Synapse Analytics dedicated SQL pool that will support multiple companies.
You need to ensure that users from each company can view only the data of their respective company.
Which two objects should you include in the solution? Each correct answer presents part of the solution.
NOTE: Each correct selection is worth one point.
A. a column encryption key
B. asymmetric keys
C. a function
D. a custom role-based access control (RBAC) role
E. a security policy

Correct Answer: C, E

242. A company is developing an end-to-end stream processing pipeline. The solution would be used to collect data for a taxi service. The taxi service would send data for each ride. The data being sent is as follows. The duration The distance The pickup and dropoff locations The solution should allow us to calculate the average tip per mile driven in real-time. Below is the architecture diagram. You have to recommend appropriate services for each stage of the architecture. Which of the following would you recommend using for Service 1?
A. Cosmos DB
B. Azure Databricks
C. Azure Event Hubs
D. Azure Functions

Correct Answer: C

243. A company is developing an end-to-end stream processing pipeline. The solution would be used to collect data for a taxi service. The taxi service would send data for each ride. The data being sent is as follows. The duration The distance The pickup and dropoff locations The solution should allow us to calculate the average tip per mile driven in real-time. Below is the architecture diagram. You have to recommend appropriate services for each stage of the architecture. Which of the following would you recommend using for Service 2?
A. Cosmos DB
B. Azure Databricks
C. Azure Event Hubs
D. Azure Functions

Correct Answer: B

244. A company is developing an end-to-end stream processing pipeline. The solution would be used to collect data for a taxi service. The taxi service would send data for each ride. The data being sent is as follows. The duration The distance The pickup and dropoff locations The solution should allow us to calculate the average tip per mile driven in real-time. Below is the architecture diagram. You have to recommend appropriate services for each stage of the architecture. Which of the following would you recommend using for Service 3?

A. Cosmos DB
B. Azure Databricks
C. Azure Event Hubs
D. Azure Functions

Correct Answer: A

245. Your company wants to set up an Azure SQL data warehouse. Data would be loaded weekly from an Azure SQL database instance. You have to advise on recommendations based on the following security requirements for the data warehouse. You have to ensure that data engineers can only connect from their on-premise workstations. You have to ensure that the right authentication and authorization measures are put in place. You have to ensure that the data is encrypted at rest. Which of the following would you recommend for the requirement? "You have to ensure data engineers can only connect from their on-premise workstations." Which of the following port must be enabled on the firewall for the data engineer's workstation?
A. 80
B. 1433
C. 3306
D. 8080

Correct Answer: B

246. Your company wants to set up an Azure SQL data warehouse. Data would be loaded weekly from an Azure SQL database instance. You have to advise on recommendations based on the following security requirements for the data warehouse. You have to ensure that data engineers can only connect from their on-premise workstations. You have to ensure that the right authentication and authorization measures are put in place. You have to ensure that the data is encrypted at rest. Which of the following would you recommend for the requirement? "You have to ensure the right authentication and authorization measures are put in place."
Which of the following technique would you use to provide authorization to the SQL data warehouse?
A. Use RBAC roles
B. Use database roles
C. Create an Azure service principal
D. Create a database firewall rule

Correct Answer: B

247. Your company wants to set up an Azure SQL data warehouse. Data would be loaded weekly from an Azure SQL database instance. You have to advise on recommendations based on the following security requirements for the data warehouse. You have to ensure data engineers can only connect from their on-premise workstations. You have to ensure the right authentication and authorization measures are put in place. You have to ensure the data is encrypted at rest. Which of the following would you recommend for the requirement? "You have to ensure the data is encrypted at rest."
A. Azure Disk Encryption
B. Transparent Data Encryption
C. SSL certificates

D. TLS Encryption

Correct Answer: B

248. A company wants to migrate a set of on-premise Microsoft SQL Server databases to Azure. Below are the requirements for each database server. whizlabsrv1 – This database server has a collection of databases that are using a set of shared resources. whizlabsrv2 – This database server is hosting a single database. The company wants to ensure a simple lift-and-shift migration for this database. whizlabsrv3 – This server hosts 2 databases. The company wants to have complete control over the underlying database server. whizlabsrv4 – This server hosts a database that has a current size of 8 TB. You have to recommend the right technology in Azure for each server ensuring costs are kept in check. Which of the following would you recommend for whizlabsrv1?
A. Azure SQL Database - Hyperscale
B. SQL Database hosted on a virtual machine
C. Azure SQL Database - Elastic pools
D. Azure SQL Database - Managed Instance

Correct Answer: C

249. A company wants to migrate a set of on-premise Microsoft SQL Server databases to Azure. Below are the requirements for each database server. whizlabsrv1 – This database server has a collection of databases that are using a set of shared resources. whizlabsrv2 – This database server is hosting a single database. The company wants to ensure a simple lift-and-shift migration for this database. whizlabsrv3 – This server hosts 2 databases. The company wants to have complete control over the underlying database server. whizlabsrv4 – This server hosts a database that has a current size of 8 TB.
You have to recommend the right technology in Azure for each server ensuring costs are kept in check. Which of the following would you recommend for whizlabsrv2?
A. Azure SQL Database - Hyperscale
B. SQL Database hosted on a virtual machine
C. Azure SQL Database - Elastic pools
D. Azure SQL Database - Managed Instance

Correct Answer: D

250. A company wants to migrate a set of on-premise Microsoft SQL Server databases to Azure. Below are the requirements for each database server. whizlabsrv1 – This database server has a collection of databases that are using a set of shared resources. whizlabsrv2 – This database server is hosting a single database. The company wants to ensure a simple lift-and-shift migration for this database.
whizlabsrv3 – This server hosts 2 databases. The company wants to have complete control over the underlying database server. whizlabsrv4 – This server hosts a database that has a current size of 8 TB. You have to recommend the right technology in Azure for each server, ensuring costs are kept in check. Which of the following would you recommend for whizlabsrv3?
A. Azure SQL Database - Hyperscale
B. SQL Database hosted on a virtual machine
C. Azure SQL Database - Elastic pools
D. Azure SQL Database - Managed Instance

Correct Answer: B

251. A company wants to migrate a set of on-premise Microsoft SQL Server databases to Azure. Below are the requirements for each database server. whizlabsrv1 – This database server has a collection of databases that are using a set of shared resources. whizlabsrv2 – This database server is hosting a single database. The company wants to ensure a simple lift-and-shift migration for this database. whizlabsrv3 – This server hosts 2 databases. The company wants to have complete control over the underlying database server. whizlabsrv4 – This server hosts a database which has a current size of 8 TB You have to recommend the right technology in Azure for each server ensuring costs are kept in check. Which of the following would you recommend for whizlabsrv4?

A. Azure SQL Database - Hyperscale

B. SQL Database hosted on a virtual machine

C. Azure SQL Database - Elastic pools

D. Azure SQL Database - Managed Instance

Correct Answer: A

ONLINE RESOURCES

Practice Paper
Link : https://forms.gle/E4vdRqxp2LzMMgUH7

QR Code:

Video Content
Link : https://www.youtube.com/playlist?list=PLzlh_31VWEFrAw_lQIMC_NlHcxi_mVUUH

QR Code:

YouTube Videos Playlists for all Microsoft Certifications Videos

Microsoft Azure AI Fundamentals AZ-900
Link: https://www.youtube.com/playlist?list=PLzlh_31VWEFq9KU8Gr0ISbfj-TW6k17f8
QR Code:

Microsoft Azure Administrator AZ-104 Microsoft Azure Virtual Desktop AZ-140
Link: https://www.youtube.com/playlist?list=PLzlh_31VWEFq7JHJMuPJZcw-XShaPrUYP
QR Code:

Microsoft Azure Virtual Desktop AZ-140
Link: https://www.youtube.com/playlist?list=PLzlh_31VWEFowmPK_ro41wiljGoGKexGI
QR Code:

Microsoft Azure Developer AZ-204

Link: https://www.youtube.com/playlist?list=PLzlh_31VWEFqT72UPVCUi6rqRqLBuwMSr

QR Code:

Designing Microsoft Azure Infrastructure Solution AZ-305

Link: https://www.youtube.com/playlist?list=PLzlh_31VWEFpTerOknh9kgL4eTbhQwDND

QR Code:

Microsoft Azure Devops Engineer AZ-400

Link: https://www.youtube.com/playlist?list=PLzlh_31VWEFpyUIe_DuaeIkcThEfMT_BT

QR Code:

Microsoft Azure Security Engineer AZ-500

Link: https://www.youtube.com/playlist?list=PLzlh_31VWEFqFBJgQTPNucIO0wVJdjNmS

QR Code:

Microsoft Azure Network Engineer AZ-700

Link: https://www.youtube.com/playlist?list=PLzlh_31VWEFowujgDl16YDCvsQtmKgEqL

QR Code:

Microsoft Azure Fundamentals AZ-900

Link: https://www.youtube.com/playlist?list=PLzlh_31VWEFpeXZ2p32R1zDsgcbV8kI1K

QR Code:

Microsoft Azure Data Engineer DP-203
Link: https://www.youtube.com/playlist?list=PLzlh_31VWEFp3XTNqoS60UAOzl8NVG-5z

QR Code:

Microsoft Azure Database Administrator DP- 300
Link: https://www.youtube.com/playlist?list=PLzlh_31VWEFpv-rmc2mbpoIqUOqVW_cIo

QR Code: